ENGLISH LANGUAGE ARTS AND READING ON THE INTERNET

A Resource for K–12 Teachers

ENGLISH LANGUAGE ARTS AND READING ON THE INTERNET

A Resource for K–12 Teachers

Jim Greenlaw
Saint Francis Xavier University

Jazlin V. Ebenezer (Series Editor)
University of Manitoba

Merrill
Prentice Hall

Upper Saddle River, New Jersey
Columbus, Ohio

Library of Congress Cataloging-in-Publication Data

Greenlaw, Jim, 1952-
  English language arts and reading on the Internet : a resource for K-12 teachers / Jim
  Greenlaw.   p.   cm.
    Includes bibliographical references.
    ISBN 0-13-020729-2
      1. Language arts--Computer-assisted instruction.   2. Reading--Computer-assisted
  instruction.   3. Internet (Computer network) in education--Directories.   I. Title.
LB1576.7 .G74 2001
428'.0078'54678--dc21   00-029800

Vice President and Publisher: Jeffery W. Johnston
Editor: Linda Ashe Montgomery
Production Editor: Mary M. Irvin
Design Coordinator: Diane C. Lorenzo
Production Coordination and Design: Clarinda Publishing Services
Cover Design: Dan Eckel
Cover Art: Diana Ong/Superstock
Production Manager: Pamela D. Bennett
Director of Marketing: Kevin Flanagan
Marketing Manager: Amy June
Marketing Services Manager: Krista Groshong

This book was set in Minion by The Clarinda Company and was printed and bound by
R. R. Donnelley & Sons Company. The cover was printed by Phoenix Color Corp.

10 9 8 7 6 5 4 3 2 1
ISBN 0-13-020729-2

For Ruth, Emily, and Colin

With love and thanks
for your patience and support

Preface

The purpose of this book is to introduce you to a selection of English language arts activities and resources that are available on the Internet's World Wide Web and to suggest ways in which you may most effectively make use of the web sites examined in the text in order to transform your teaching of reading, writing, speaking, listening, and viewing. Because you may not have had much experience at using various search engines such as Yahoo and AltaVista to find English teaching sites and materials on the Internet, our first chapter is devoted to explaining how such searches can be carried out. We also describe some of the electronic journals, professional organizations, and lesson plan sites that might be most fruitful. After this we describe the info-bar that will be used in Chapters 4 and 5 to summarize key features of the sites we are evaluating in terms of their intended audience, grade level, curricular fit, types of resources, site authorship, navigation, visual appeal, and interactive activities.

In Chapter 2 we discuss some of the recently developed theories about hypertextuality that form a necessary foundation for our explanation of the changes that technology is causing in K–12 language arts classrooms. To illustrate in concrete terms how these theories apply to actual teaching situations, we provide you with nine models of effective and imaginative uses of the Internet to teach language arts to your students.

In the third chapter we focus on recent research in the teaching of reading. We survey a variety of sites that offer you and your students excellent reading materials and lessons. Chapter 4 enables you to identify at a glance the strengths and weaknesses of many literature sites. In this chapter we review, for example, sites that contain information and activities intended to make the study of children's literature, young adult literature, mythology, poetry, short stories, novels, and drama more interesting and enjoyable for your students.

Finally, in Chapter 5, we examine the standards of the National Council of Teachers of English and the International Reading Association for evaluating student learning in K–12 English language arts courses. Then we explain how a variety of Internet sites can help you to enable your students to develop their knowledge of literature and their understanding of the writing process. These web sites can assist your students in their attempts to research the history of English literature, receive constructive criticism from writers in electronic residence, take part in online grammar activities, write for newspapers and magazines, write speeches and e-mail, study English as a second language, compare English to other languages, and develop critical media literacy skills for studying newspapers, magazines, and film.

At the end of each chapter, so that you can more fully appreciate the power of the sites that we include, we have listed a number of activities for you to try. As well, in an appendix at the end of the book, we provide an Internet glossary for easing surfing.

Our primary goal in writing this book is to familiarize you with as many useful web sites and teaching strategies as possible. While guiding you through the many fascinating texts and activities that these sites have to offer, we hope at the same time to engage you in a conversation about the nature of knowledge construction in cyberspace so that you can reflect upon what is worthwhile and rewarding for you and your students in the study of English language arts on the Internet.

We would like to thank the reviewers of this text for their insights and comments: Cathy Block, Texas Christian University; Ward A. Cockrum, Northern Arizona University; Claudia Cornett, Wittenberg University; Patricia P. Fritchie, Troy State University-Dothan; and Leanna Manna, Villa Maria College.

Contents

CHAPTER 4 ■ *Literature for Children and Adolescents 51*

CHAPTER 5 ■ *Language Arts Standards and Activities 118*

Glossary

CHAPTER 1

Untangling the Web

- The Significance of the Internet for Teachers
- Surfing the Internet
- Sites for Internet Guides and Tutorials
- Resources for Reading and Language Arts Teachers
- Criteria for Evaluating Materials

THE SIGNIFICANCE OF THE INTERNET FOR TEACHERS

Whether you are a student teacher learning about the complexities of language arts pedagogy for the first time, or an experienced English educator interested in adding technological teaching components, you will find many useful and fascinating Internet sites that have mainly been developed by educators such as yourself. Perhaps you would like to download information about how to use puppets with your kindergarten students, or you hope to find music from India and Japan to add to your grade 3 integrated multicultural theme unit. You might wish to discover audio clips of Robert Frost's poetry for your grade 7 students to use in their multimedia anthologies, or videoclips of actors performing Shakespeare for your grade 10 drama class. Then again, you may want to make a virtual visit to the home pages of schools in Australia, South Africa, and Hong Kong with the teachers there to connect their students with yours to conduct intercultural collaborative writing projects together.

Your students' parents, the technology coordinators at your local district school board office, the government department of education computer consultants, and, of course, your students now all expect you to follow language arts curriculum guide objectives that stress technological competence as a basic literacy skill at the beginning of the twenty-first century. You have probably used an Internet browser such as Netscape to look up books on Amazon.com, and it is likely that before reading this book you have written e-mail to friends in other parts of Canada and the United States. Perhaps you have even done some serious web page construction and searched for lesson plans to use with your students. Regardless of your background knowledge, you will find the resources in this book to be helpful to you in your important job as a literacy worker.

If you were teaching language arts just a few years ago, you probably considered yourself lucky to be able to bring your class into a computer lab once a week to involve them in some basic word processing activities. If you did have access to the Internet, you may have found some information that was interesting to you personally but not of much value to you as a teacher. Yet now, you are probably expected to give your students regular and frequent assignments on computers. You have found so many sites on the Internet that are useful to you as a reading teacher that you could spend 24 hours a day trying to visit them all and hardly scratch the surface. Given the rapid rate of change in this field, it is difficult to imagine what technocultural trends and literacy lessons will be a part of teachers' lives a decade from now. But there is not doubt that for years to come language arts teachers will continue to be indispensible in helping disabled and gifted, English-as-a-second-language (ESL) and cultural minority students to read and write texts, and technological understanding is sure to continue as a significant factor in English educators' lives.

This first chapter provides basic information about the Internet before moving on to the contents of language arts and reading sites. If you are quite an expert at finding your way around the World Wide Web but have not had the opportunity to spend time looking for good sites to use in your teaching, then proceed now to the second half of this chapter to read about Internet resources for reading and language arts teachers.

SURFING THE INTERNET

The Internet is a huge network of interconnected computer networks linking the whole world. For example, the computers in a college of education can be linked to form a network of computers. This is what is known as a *LAN (local area network)*. This single network of computers is connected to other colleges in the same university, and the university computer network is then connected to a series of networks in other universities, school networks, commercial and business networks, government networks, industry networks, and many other networks throughout the world that transcend geographical barriers. All of the computer networks have multilevel connections with telephones and satellites. Intercontinental telephone and fiber optic connection lines run beneath the ocean floor to link all the continents.

An increasing number of websites is added each day to the Internet, making it more and more difficult to find relevant information. The emergence of search engines and search directories, however, has harnessed the overflow of websites. With definitive subject and topic *keywords* (words used by the search engines), information and resources on the Internet can be more quickly located and extracted. The Netscape browser provides a "graphic interface to the Internet and the World Wide Web allowing for exploration of information via hot buttons which link to further resources" (Morris, 1996).

Each computer on the Internet is tagged, or personalized, with a set of numbers or letters known as the *IP (Internet Protocol) address*. The IP address enables you to search, locate, and connect to a specific computer that provides the information for which you are looking. To find a website on the Internet, a particular *syntax,* or arrangement of information, must be used to reach the "address" of the other computer. This Internet website address is called a *URL,* which stands for *Uniform Resource Locator.* An example of a URL for a website is

http://www.scils.rutgers.edu/special/kay/kayhp2.html

The standard format for a URL is *protocol://host.domain[:port][/path][filename]* in which

- ■ The *protocol* is http (HyperText Transport Protocol) for an http type of information server.
- ■ The *host.domain* is a reference to the server (www.scils.rutgers.edu).
- ■ The *path* is a reference to the website on the server(/special/kay/).
- ■ The *filename* refers to a file in the site (kayhp2.html).

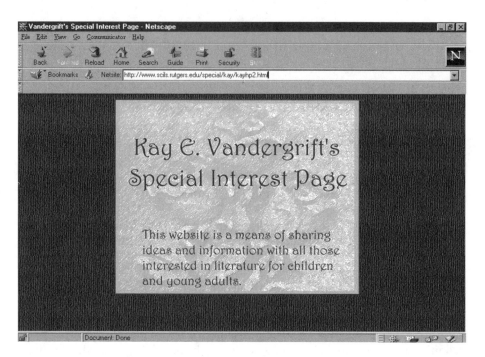

This standard format, or syntax, allows the browser client software to recognize and to make the appropriate connections to the location of the websites. It operates in a manner somewhat similar to telephone or postal codes.

Most language arts teachers are familiar with how to conduct a basic Internet search with the Netscape browser, so this chapter will simply provide a few suggestions to make searches more fruitful. Traditional search engines (that is, engines that have been operating for more than a few years), such as Yahoo, contain links to hundreds of thousands of sites for many of the terms that you might enter. For instance, when we recently typed in the search term "children's literature" on AltaVista we encountered 37,457 "hits," or site references containing these words. By the time you read this book the number of sites will undoubtedly have grown. But when we used the Education K–12 menu on Yahoo and chose the category of *Children's Reading Lists,* we discovered a short collection of 12 reasonably useful sites. Our point here is simple. There is already far more information on the Internet about teaching language arts than anyone could ever possibly use, and much of it is not worth reading. Moreover, what is good is often difficult to find. So you need to develop strategies for narrowing your searches. Look for menus like those under the *Reading* category in Yahoo. Once you have found a good site (such as the ones listed in the following pages of this book), often it is linked to other sites that may be of interest to you and your students. Also, instead of entering broad search terms such as "children's literature," try to be more specific by using the name of an author, "Beverly Cleary," a book, "The Cat in the Hat," or a teaching method, "Creative Drama," and you are more likely to find shorter lists of sites which may be of use to you.

SITES FOR INTERNET GUIDES AND TUTORIALS

Guides and tutorials that will assist you in surfing the Internet can be obtained at the following URLs.

Internet Web Text (Index)

For a collection of most of the guides and tutorials that are available on the Internet, see

http://www.december.com/web/text/index.html

Internet Guides, Tutorials, and Training Information

Explore and download some of the documents that this library of Internet guides and tutorials offers. Make sure you download the latest documents to get up-to-date information.

http://www.loc.gov/global/internet/training.html

Internet 101

The following website provides the basics on using the Net and includes tips on searching, e-mail, newsgroups, and chat rooms.

http://www2.famvid.com/i101/

Jay Barker's Online Connection

To compare the major U.S. Internet service providers based on their speed, price, software, features, and support, see

http://www.barkers.org/online/

Life on the Internet

This beginners' guide gives over 300 links as well as tips on using the browsers.

http://www.screen.com/start/welcome.html

Netscape's Homepage

At Netscape's homesite, you can download Netscape's newest browsers. You can also get Net tutorials and references at this site.

http://home.netscape.com/

New Surfer's Guide

For helpful articles on how to tour the Web and understand the terms used, plus access to some useful starting points, see

http://www.imagescape.com/helpweb/www/oneweb.html

Sites to See

Resources and handouts from this introductory hands-on WWW workshop are available. Material covers Web navigation and surfing.

http://www.wolinskyweb.com/jintro.htm

The Internet Help Desk

This free guide helps both beginners and advanced Internet users. Material covers e-mail, netiquette, and browsers.

http://w3.one.net/~alward/

The Online World Resources Handbook

Help with starting points, web page design, e-mail, and other facets of the Web can be found at this webstite.

http://www.simtel.net/simtel.net/presno/bok/

RESOURCES FOR READING AND LANGUAGE ARTS TEACHERS

The following is just a brief sampling of some of the many sites that, because they attempt to provide K–12 English teachers access to a wide variety of resources, are good places for you to begin your search for interesting language arts materials, resources, lesson plans, and professional information. As you navigate through these sites looking for other linked sites that may be useful to you and your students, you can keep track of those sites that interest you by clicking on the Bookmark button in Netscape. *Bookmarking* enables you to keep a list of favorite sites. Then, the next time you wish to visit these sites, you simply open your list of bookmarks and click on the name of the site you want. Netscape will take you right there. The first few sites described here contain literally hundreds of carefully organized links to language arts resources worldwide.

ERIC Clearinghouse on Reading, English and Communication

http://www.indiana.edu/~eric_rec/

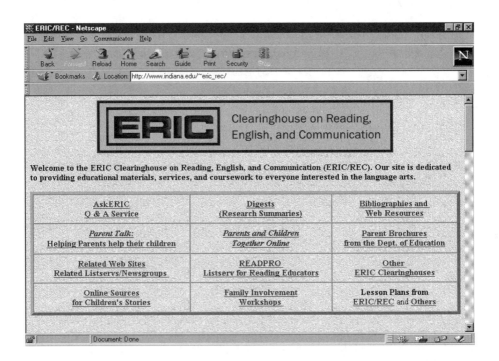

The *ERIC Clearinghouse on Reading, English, and Communication* provides a wealth of links to lesson plans, bibliographies and Web resources as well as *listservs* on which you can learn more about elementary and secondary language arts by corresponding via e-mail with fellow English teachers. In its *Online Sources for Children's Stories* section you can find links to a number of excellent sites that we describe in Chapter 3, such as *Kidpub, Tales of Wonder,* and *The Children's Literature Web Guide.* And in its *Related Web Sites* section you can find sites concerned with *Theatre and Drama, Journalism, Poetry, Storytelling,* and *Book Reviews,* to name just a few categories.

ISLMC Children's Literature and Language Arts Resources

http://falcon.jmu.edu/~ramseyil/childlit.htm

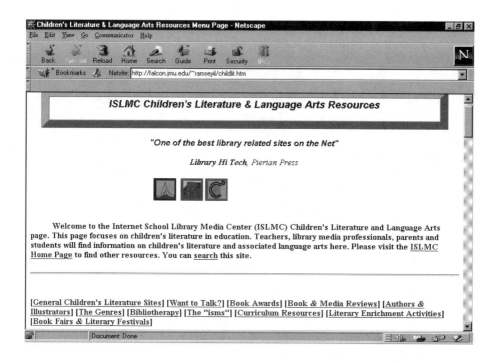

The Internet School Library Media Centre (ISLMC) has developed a site called the *Children's Literature and Language Arts Resources* page that contains links to a wonderful assortment of children's literature sites, chat rooms, keypal organizations, curriculum resources, and enrichment activities. Among the noteworthy links from this site are *Young Adult Literature, Children's and YA Book/Media Awards, Authors and Illustrators, Biography/Autobiography, Multicultural Education Resources, Nonfiction, Picture Books, Series Books, Bibliotherapy, Families in Children's Literature, Spirituality in Kids' Books, Curriculum Units, ESL, Gifted Education, Literacy, Teaching Reading, Creative Dramatics,* and *Music and Songs.* Through each of these links you will have access to hundreds of excellent sites such as *KidsCom, Author Biographies for Middle and Secondary Students, Internet Research Project Student Resources, Multicultural Book Reviews, Historical Fiction Bibliographies,* and *The On-Line Visual Literacy Project.*

The English Server

http://eserver.org/

Another very interesting and useful place for you to consider as a starting point in your explorations of English sites is *The English Server*. This site was created by the English Department of Carnegie Mellon University for university English students and professors, but many of the sites to which this server is linked are of great value to elementary and secondary school English teachers as well. For instance, in its *Fiction* section you can find electronic versions of works by and about such novelists as the Brontes, Dickens, Defoe, and Conrad. The works of poets, dramatists, and journalists are also available in electronic texts. Related categories within this site include *Cultural Theory, Film and Television, Feminism, Art and Architecture,* and *Community Literacy.*

NCTE National Council of Teachers of English

http://www.ncte.org/

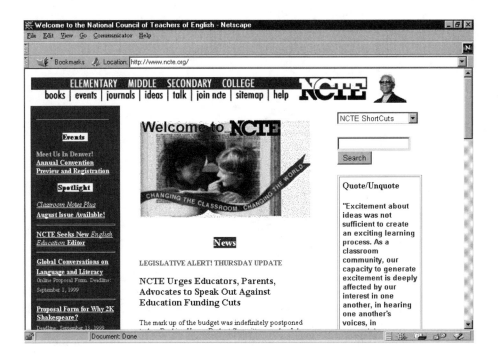

The *National Council of Teachers of English* (NCTE) home page contains a wealth of information about English teaching ideas, standards, journals, jobs, research, teacher preparation, professional development, and discussion lists. If you want to order NCTE books on assessment, literacy, whole-language, reading, and computers and technology, you will find their paragraph descriptions of these texts helpful. Some of the journals that can be ordered through this site are *English Education, Primary Voices K–6, Voices from the Middle, Research in the Teaching of English, English Journal,* and *Language Arts.*

The Internet TESL Journal

http://www.aitech.ac.jp/~iteslj/

The Internet TESL Journal is a monthly publication that has been available on the World Wide Web since 1995. Because you can access back issues of this journal, you may download an amazing assortment of lessons and teaching ideas from this site. Or you can use the journal's own search engine to view 3,700 other ESL sites on the Internet. You can also read numerous articles and research papers, or you can view a variety of projects under such headings as conversation questions, jokes, games, and activities. This site is an essential starting point for teachers and students of ESL and EFL.

Reading Online

http://www.readingonline.org/home.html

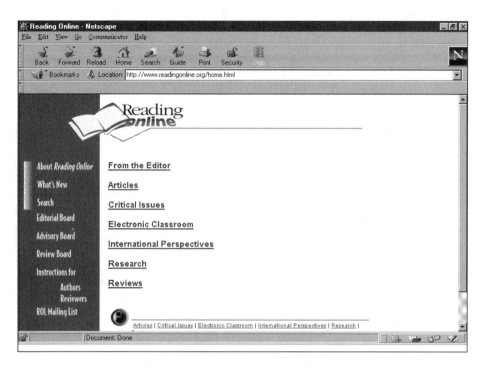

Reading Online is an electronic journal of the International Reading Association. Its contributers include K–12 reading teachers and teacher educators. The articles are nicely organized in *hypertext* format so that you can, for example, click on the title of a book being discussed by the article's author and move immediately to a description of that book on an ERIC database. After you finish reading the article, you are encouraged by the journal's editors to take part in an online discussion forum about the issues it raises. In the *International Perspectives* section of the journal you can read, for example, an article about research on literacy in Malaysia, and in the *Electronic Classroom* section you can read an article titled "Technology and the Revival of the Hawaiian Language."

CRITERIA FOR EVALUATING MATERIALS

Web-searching tools such as *Netscape* and *Internet Explorer* have made searching and publishing on the Internet very easy. Therefore, new websites are continually being added. Now, in the year 2000, there are an estimated 148 million English native speakers using the Internet and another 128 million non-English speakers on the Internet (*Global Internet Statistics,* http://www.euromktg.com/globstats/).

At least 10 search engines are available, but we found *Altavista, Excite, Magellan,* and *Yahoo* to be the most important for English education. For every hit with each search engine, there are over 5,000 sites on a given topic of research, making it impossible to go through all the sites. We usually visited up to 40 sites plus the links for the categories and subcategories. Although some sites sounded very exciting, when we opened them, the message was a disappointing, "File Not Found. . . . The requested URL was not found on the server." Most often, only one out of every 20 sites is "Networthy." Hence, searching is time-consuming, often frustrating, and requires patience. Teachers must overcome these obstacles to use the Internet meaningfully and help our students do the same. Following is a list of criteria for the selection of resources on the Internet:

1. The lesson plan on the Internet should match the objectives and outcomes of your department of education's curriculum.

2. English content of an activity should be at the appropriate developmental level.

3. Reading level should be grade and age appropriate.

4. Meaningful information and activities for both teachers and students should be presented.

5. Lesson plans and activities should reflect critical thinking; constructivism; integration of reading, writing, speaking, listening, viewing, and representing; and multiple approaches to teaching and learning.

6. Links to other related websites should be provided.

7. Background information should be included with lesson plans.

8. Connections to experts, peers, teachers, or mailing lists should be provided.

9. Activities should be online or downloadable to local disks.

10. Information should be presented with a multimedia approach—sound, animation, and aesthetically pleasing graphics.

11. Articles and papers should include complete references.

We have surfed through many websites in language arts and reading education, and, based upon the preceeding criteria, we have selected sites that are useful for both teachers and students. But the reader should also surf through these sites before recommending them to students.

The Internet can be incorporated easily into English teaching and learning. It offers both practical (providing information and activities) and theoretical (collaborating and construction) values as well as a shift in power from the teacher to the students.

In Chapters 3, 4, and 5 we have brought together an annotated collection of websites providing a variety of resources for teaching reading and English language arts. Our intent is to offer you a broad sampling of the many Internet sites that contain resources for teaching English. The sites included in Chapter 3 focus upon research and lesson plans for teachers of reading. Chapter 4 includes a multitude of sites about the kinds of literature and authors taught in K–12 classrooms. And the language arts sites we provide for you in Chapter 5 have been selected to correspond to the NCTE and IRA standards for English language arts that we present at the beginning of the chapter. The sites in Chapter 5 are organized into the following categories: English Language Arts Standards, Researching the History of the English Literature, Grammar On-Line, Publishing and Exploring Student Writing, Writing Newspapers and Magazines, Debating and Speech Writing, Composing and Sharing of Multimedia Presentations, English as a Second Language Projects and Resources, Intercultural Commnication Via Email, Comparing Other Languages with English, Creating School Home Pages, Newspapers and Magazines, Radio, Television, and Film.

The assessment of the grade-level suitability of the resources contained at a site is best seen as an approximate guide for several reasons. The resources often can be applied to a number of grade-levels. The authors of the sites sometimes state the intended grade level, but often they do not. The grade-level suitability of concepts and skills included in curriculum documents is determined largely by state and provincial education authorities. There is no universal agreement on these issues. And, of course, the readiness to learn of students must also be taken into account when determining grade-level suitability.

Useful information is provided for each listed site: its title and URL, a description of its pertinent features, and a profile consisting of eight components:

1. *Intended audience:* Teachers, teachers and students, or just students.
2. *Grade level:* One or more grades from K–12.
3. *Curricular fit:* For example, creative writing and drama in the English and theater arts class.
4. *Type of resources:* For example, links to various worthwhile ESL project sites.
5. *Authorship of site:* Commercial enterprise, university/school, government agency, professional organization, or private individual.
6. *Navigation:* Satisfactory, good, or very good.
7. *Visual appeal:* Satisfactory, good, or very good.
8. *Interactive activity:* For example, some opportunity to take part in discussion groups.

For most of the sites in Chapters 4 and 5 we have organized the preceding information in the following chart form:

http://	
Intended Audience	
Grade Level	
Curricular Fit	
Types of Resources	
Authorship of Site	
Navigation	
Visual Appeal	
Interactive Activity	

Intended audience refers to the audience (teachers, students, or both) who would benefit most from the material found at the site. *Grade level* refers to the recommended grade level or levels for the material found at the site. *Curricular fit* refers to the main English areas/topics that the site addresses (e.g., grammar, young adult literature, etc.). *Type of resources* refers to whether the site is a collection of links to other sites (a *gateway* site) or a storehouse of specific content (e.g., puppetry activities, E-text of British literature, etc.), or both. *Authorship of site* refers to the creator of the site (i.e., a private individual, a university, or some other type of organization). *Navigation* refers to how simple and convenient it is for the user to access various parts of the site.

Visual appeal refers to how well the site might capture the user's interest because of the way the site is organized and the extent to which graphics and special effects are used. Visual appeal likely has the most relevance for sites that are intended for students. It also provides a rough measure of the display speed of a site, because a site with very good visual appeal tends to be graphics-rich in the design of its web pages. This kind of site will have a slower display speed, while a site with minimal graphics will have a faster display speed.

Interactive Activity refers to the extent of interaction that is possible between the user and the site's resources. The word "None" means that all the user can do is read and look at pictures or go to other links. If, on the other hand, students may leave copies of their writing at a site, become involved in discussion groups, listen to a famous poet reading his poetry, etc., then we usually describe in a phrase the pertinent activities.

SUGGESTED ACTIVITIES

1. Choose a search term such as "multicultural literature," "whole language," or "ESL," and compare the results with several different search engines such as Yahoo, AltaVista, and Google.

2. Visit one of the professional organization sites listed in this chapter and subscribe to a teachers' newsgroup. After you read a sampling from the group's archives, submit a question to the group or contact one of the individuals who has raised an issue that interests you.

3. Visit the ISLMC Children's Literature or the TESL site, and follow its links to other related sites.

4. Use the criteria for evaluating websites that are provided in this chapter to assess the quality of some of the children's literature author sites listed on the ISLMC site.

5. Create two criteria of your own for evaluating Internet sites.

6. Consider a research question you would like to ask about reading, writing, student learning difficulties, etc., then visit the ERIC site to search its research digests in order to see what some reading and language arts education experts have discovered thus far in answer to your question.

SUMMARY

We have described what the Internet is and have shown you how to surf the Internet. For detailed procedures on surfing, we have referred you to a number of sites where guides and tutorials are available. In this chapter we have also introduced you to a few general English language arts sites. Our hope is that, with the assistance provided here, you will not become discouraged by the vast amount of information that you discover, but will use the helpful hints from this chapter to become an efficient and discerning Internet user. Happy surfing!

REFERENCES

Morris, J. L. (1996). *The Technology Revolution.*
http://www.uvm.edu/~jmoris/comps2.html
Savetz, K. (1996). *The un-official Internet book list: Site indices & guides—Education.*
http://www.northcoast.com/savetz/booklist/education.html

CHAPTER 2

English Education Reform in a Technological World

- Reform through Technology
- Models for Internet Teaching
- Role of the Teacher
- K–12 Reading and Language Arts Sites

REFORM THROUGH TECHNOLOGY

Intellectual and communicative processes are integral to constructing and negotiating knowledge in the English language arts. Students need to be able to find evidence in texts to support their interpretations of literature. They must be able to generate their own questions about literature and propose possible answers. An English class should reflect the beginnings of the creative and critical aspects of literacy that the students will need to possess in their adult life.

In technologically rich societies such as the United States and Canada, *hypertextual reading* and writing skills and *lateral thinking* abilities are necessary components of literacy development. In his book, *Hypertext 2.0: The Convergence of Contemporary Critical Theory and Technology* (1997), George Landow suggests that hypertext's "emphasis upon the active, empowered reader, which fundamentally calls into question general assumptions about reading, writing, and texts, similarly calls into question our assumptions about the nature and institutions of literary education that so depend upon these texts" (p. 219).

Hypermedia and hypertextual sites on the Internet can provide wonderful opportunities for students to learn about the aesthetic features of literary texts. Through intercultural communication and through the exploration of cultural background materials, they can also learn from multiple perspectives about cultural representations of themselves and others.

Developments in cognitive and social psychology as well as technology in the last decade have provided new perspectives on learning. These new perspectives have contributed to the systemic reform of school curricula and ways of teaching and assessing instruction. Learning is presently viewed as personal, social, and situational. It also depends upon the attitudes, values, and interests of the learner. In line with these new developments, English education is focusing on lifelong learning and skill development that will enable students to inquire, construct new ideas, wrestle with complexity, cope with uncertainty and ambiguity, adapt to constant change, solve conventional and unconventional problems, and develop a high degree of interpersonal and intrapersonal competence.

Christopher Dede, a professor of information technology, argues that new technological developments can help transform schools if these developments are used to support new models of teaching and learning, models that characterize sustained, community-centered, constructivist classrooms for learner investigation, collaboration, and construction (O'Neil, 1995). The Internet can promote a collaborative culture in "doing English." For example, Jim Cummins and Dennis Sayers, in their book, *Brave New Schools: Challenging Cultural Literacy Through Global Learning Networks* (1995), have proposed that in order to avoid monocultural prescriptions for educational reform, teachers should establish "long-distance teaching partnerships across cultures, intercultural networks of partnerships that—to the greatest extent feasible—seek to take advantage of accessible and culturally appropriate educational and communications technology" (p. 11). In other words, they believe that teachers should use the Internet for intercultural communication if they want to (1) include such content and skills in their curricula as global education, literacy development, critical thinking, and second-language learning and (2) at the same time promote sensitivity to other cultural perspectives and to stimulate their students' research skill development. However, Cummins and Sayers also point out that, "as with any innovation in education—without an overarching conception of how to shape learning in the direction of the sort of critical inquiry that prepares our youth for the future, the global learning networks will merely lead to trivializing, superficial classroom practices that do little to reverse patterns of student, teacher, and community disempowerment" (p. 80).

MODELS FOR INTERNET TEACHING

In the past, teachers shaped children's conceptions about reading and writing literature and literary criticism by means of authorized, or prescribed, language arts textbooks. But the Internet has now become a major force in shaping young minds, and teachers who use Internet technology in their classrooms know the potential benefits it brings to the overall learning of their students.

How can you teach in a knowledge-intensive society? This is a challenge for most teachers—a reason we turn to computers and the Information Superhighway. When they graduate, young people are expected to be fluent in information literacy skills in the workplace. English education is the appropriate context for many of these skills to be developed. The online world enables children to explore a new set of experiences and helps them to satisfy their curiosity. Through experts' knowledge, the Internet can provide answers to questions that children ask.

What are the potential uses of the Internet in a language arts classroom? In the following section we present nine models to indicate just a few of the imaginative ways in which English teachers can expose their students to interactive learning experiences on the Internet.

Model 1: Collaborative Story Writing Across the Globe

In 1997 Deborah Falk, at Duck Bay School in Manitoba, posted the following project proposal on the Internet:

> I am looking to organize a story writing project with interested schools. The way the project will work is that six schools will work together to write a story. When you register your class, I will form a Story Writing Group for you and five other classes. Each class will be assigned a one-week period in which to write their paragraph and email it to me during the assigned week. I will then send that paragraph to class two, who will write paragraph two, and so on . . . until the story is completed with paragraph 6. The reason that you will send the paragraph to me is so that I can forward the paragraph to all classes in your story group. I am combining geography with language arts.

Deborah also told the participating teachers in the project that there would be two groups of stories: those written for and by grade 1–4 students and those written by and for grade 5–8 students. After the stories were completed Deborah had enabled more than 250 students from the United States, Canada, Australia, and the United Kingdom to take part in the writing of 43 delightful stories, which you can read by visiting her project site at

http://www.mbnet.mb.ca/~dfalk/story2.html.

Deborah's project demonstrated at least two of the virtues of a well-conceived Internet activity. The students had an opportunity to share their story ideas with other students around the world. They wrote with a group of international peers as their authentic audience. Also, they could see where their fellow writers lived on an online map of the world, so they learned about other countries as part of their assignment.

In another collaborative story writing project, grade 4 teachers Carla Churchulla of Maryland, Hanne Bentzen of Denmark, and Carolyn Brutan of South Africa, with the help of project facilitator, John Ost, enabled their students to collaborate on the Internet in order to write a multimedia novel titled *The Oil Spill Mystery*. You can read the novel and follow its links to related sites yourself by visiting the children's Kidlink project site at

http://www.kidlink.org/KIDPROJ/Kidwriters/Mystery/Maryland/index.html.

The teachers first heard about the project through an e-mail message on the Kidlink listserv. In order to coordinate their students' writing efforts they frequently had to send messages to each other using e-mail because of the time zone differences. The students in Denmark, for instance, were out of school before the Maryland students had awakened in the morning.

John Ost of New Hampshire met with the students online at least once a week to guide them in their writing. The classes created committees to handle different aspects of the project. They conducted regular committee meetings and wrote logs of their activities. The Writers Committee was in charge of adding ideas to the story once they had received input from all three classes. The Illustrator Committee was in charge of creating the illustrations for each scene of the story. The Mathematicians Committee created the math problems that were integrated into the story as it progressed. And the Researchers Committee carried out Internet searches to be sure that the facts of their story were true. For instance, they checked whether or not an eagle can fly across the ocean. They also checked out some facts about sea monsters. The Web Designers Committee learned how to create a web page and were responsible for designing the pages for their mystery. Finally, the Communicators Committee was responsible for writing e-mail messages to the students in the other two countries.

The resulting novel contained a really good, mysterious plot. The enthusiastically rendered illustrations were scanned into the computer and interspersed throughout the story. The web designers and reseachers provided links to related sites on oil spills and sea monsters. As in the first case study discussed in this chapter (Deborah Falk's project), this one indicates some very creative thinking. E-mail communication, Internet research, web page design and construction, drawing and scanning of art work, and overall coordination of the group activities resulted in a rich and pleasurable learning experience for the participants. Furthermore, some delightful and instructive reading material was provided for other grade 4 students around the world.

Model 2: Reading between Worlds—Intercultural Literary Interpretation

This project involved grade 10 Chinese-Canadian students in Vancouver communicating via e-mail with bilingual Japanese students in Kyoto to share their interpretations of a Japanese short story in English translation (Greenlaw, 1992). To begin the project the students were encouraged to become acquainted with each other through introductory messages. During these interchanges the students shared information about their schools and communities. For example, the Kyoto students pointed out that their school is located in the country, about 20 minutes from Kyoto Station, and that "Kyoto is one of the cities in Japan left with historical sites, such as famous temples and shrines that people from all over the world come to visit." They noted as well that they "enjoy shopping, talking with friends and other things" that their key pals would do in Vancouver.

During this introduction period the students were a little surprised, in fact, to discover how much they had in common with their key pals. For example, in Vancouver, Jennifer said, "I told [Masae] about my interests in acting and singing and it just happened that she was interested in the same things as me." While in the early stages it was beneficial for the students to establish a sense of common interests and concerns, as they came to know each other better, their pleasure in discussing cultural differences also grew.

At the same time that the students were becoming acquainted with each other through these personal exchanges, they also learned more about each other by sharing their interpretations of the short story, "Spring Storm" by Mori Yoko. Most of the students felt that this Japanese story provided a good starting point for their discussions about Japanese and North American culture. The story concerns a critical moment in the relationship between the actress Midori Natsuo and her husband, script writer Asai Yusuke. On the day when Midori learns, much to her surprise, that she has been chosen to be the star of a musical, she also gradually comes to realize that her husband cannot accept her new career status because he feels it would diminish his own. As Mori Yoko's narrative unfolds, we see Midori's developing awareness of her predicament, first in her confused feelings of intense joy and suffocating pain while she approaches their apartment, then in her mistrust as she attempts to conceal the truth from Yusuke, and finally in her recognition of the choice that she must inevitably make between her marriage and her career.

In the following interchange with Jennifer concerning "Spring Storm," Masae's explanation of the meaning of the storm and blossoms indicated that she possessed a strong grasp of the theme of gender inequity as it was revealed to her through the story's symbolism:

This story probably got its title from the part where Midori and Yusuke talk about the storm and the cherry blossoms. When I read this story, I interpreted that the cherry blossoms were intended to symbolize women trying to "blossom" out into what was known up until then as the "men's world." The storm shows the men's discriminatory ideas against women, standing in their way and not letting them blossom. You can tell from what Yusuke says, that once the storm "stops," more women will be involved in the world. Midori's reply of how there will be more storms explains, in a way, that there will be more obstacles for women before they can really blossom.

At the end of the project the students in Kyoto and Vancouver each expressed their opinions about the process they had experienced. In Vancouver, Jennifer offered the following concluding remarks about "Spring Storm":

Masae said that Japanese culture was very much like it was in "Spring Storm." The women are supposed to stay at home. They're not supposed to go out into the business world because it's a man's world. She said that now they are starting to break away from that.

And, in Japan, Masae's remarks indicated that through her dialogue with Jennifer she had come to think about the story from an intercultural perspective:

In Japanese magazines for teens you read that guys hate girls who are smarter than them. In "Spring Storm" Usuke couldn't stand Midori earning more money than him. It's up to the individual person. I think our society has been stereotyped. My Dad helps out in the house now more than he used to. I wouldn't want to marry a guy who says that I have to stay at home and do housework. I'd probably give up working if I had a child, but, if not, I'd want to keep on working.

Model 3: Using Professional Writers and Senior Citizens as Mentors

There are many fine sites on the Internet devoted to teaching high school students how to write, but one of the most successful in terms of the opportunities it offers students to gain guidance from professional writers is the *Writers in Electronic Residence (WIER)* site (http://www.edu.yorku.ca/WIERHome/). This site is run out of York University in Toronto by its founder, Trevor Owen. Over the past decade over 20,000 students in 300 schools have been aided in their writing by some 40 professional authors. The program has also facilitated the learning of writing skills by connecting students with teachers and with each other. The WIER site is well worth visiting as well in order to access for free the list of *Cool Tools for Online Writing,* which includes electronic versions of *Roget's Thesaurus* and *Webster's Dictionary.*

One significant aspect of WIER is Owen's recommendation that when students are working with their peers and mentors on their writing, all of their texts be printed out and stored in binders for further reflection to avoid the students focusing more on the technology than on the writing. Owen's point is an important one.

Interactivity does not mean that students must remain glued to their computer screens as if they were playing a video game. They can certainly benefit by taking their peers' writing or their own work away from the computer to revise it in groups with pen in hand. In the same way, if they download an audio file of a speech or a piece of music, they can tape record it or save it onto a disk to study at their own pace at home.

A variation on the WIER mentoring model could involve connecting K–6 students with senior citizens who would enjoy giving the youngsters the positive feedback they need to inspire them to write more stories, poems, and project reports.

Model 4: Sharing Your School Community with Others

As you will learn in Chapter 5, through the Web66 International School Web Site Registry site (**http://web66.coled.umn.edu/schools.html**), it is possible to visit the home pages of thousands of schools around the world. When you do this you will discover that many of these schools have made efforts to introduce visitors to their staff members, students, and surrounding communities. If your school already has an active home page, we recommend that you consider using it as a site for publishing your students audio, photographic, and written essays and stories about themselves, their school, and their community.

The students of Peerless Lake School, 500 miles north of Edmonton in Alberta, for example, have published a number of articles about their interests in snowmobiling, fur trapping, and floor hockey. Visitors to their school's home page can also read about an Internet project they experienced in partnership with schools in Japan and Sweden. Or they can read about the film which was made in their community about two of the school's students who won an award for bravery after they rescued some children from a burning house.

At the Austin E. Lathrop School site in Alaska, you can read biographies of some of the school's students and you can send e-mail messages to them. If you want to learn about the Gwich'in Athabascan culture, you can go to the linked page at the site about the Athabascan Indians and read a research paper on the subject written by one of the school's students. Sites such as these, which you may discover on Web66, can serve as models for the work your students produce to share their community with the world.

Model 5: Taking Internet Field Trips

Each April or May since 1990 all of the seventh grade students at Hong Kong International School have made a trip into Mainland China to experience Chinese culture first-hand. Since 1995, through descriptive writing and photographs, the visitors from Hong Kong have been sharing with interested students around the world impressions of their trip to Xi'an in a project they call *Virtual China* (**http://www.kidlink.org/KIDPROJ/vchina99/**). This particular Internet project is interesting for a number of reasons. If your middle school students want to study China from the perspective of fellow adolescents, the entries by the students in

Hong Kong are very well-written and informative. Also, if your students want to learn more about the topics discussed by the grade 7 classes in Hong Kong, there is a bulletin board at which they can leave questions to be answered by the Hong Kong students. But more importantly, this project can provide a model for your own students to make reports on similar field trips into their own regions and to share their findings with students in other parts of the United States and Canada or in other countries.

The method the Hong Kong students used to publish their research is quite simple to reproduce if your school has a home page. Using a scanner and software such as *Word for Office 97,* your students can type in their reports and scan in their photographs and then hyperlink their work to a specially designated *Web Project Page* on your school's home page. Then, when students from other schools visit this *Web Project Page* and leave questions, the perfect opportunity exists to begin a dialogue with the visitors comparing their region and yours.

Model 6: Researching and Constructing Thematic Multimedia Projects

One of the best ways that you and your students can make effective use of the Internet's unique power is to employ *multimedia* (sound and animation). In order to learn more about the technical aspects of multimedia production, you should visit the site titled *Introduction to Multimedia: An Overview for Educators* (**http:// cee.indiana.edu/publications/multipres/MM.html**). Our suggestions in this model are primarily concerned with using the multimedia sites that other educators have created to make your students' Internet learning activities as hypertextually significant and attractive as possible. But we hope that after you encounter a few of these sites, you will be inspired to produce with your students your own multimedia Internet projects. The software and hardware that now exist for such productions are very user-friendly. If your school already possesses a few computers with an Internet connection, then the additional cost for items such as a basic image scanner should not prove excessive.

One well-conceived and imaginatively structured multimedia site that could inspire your students to carry out a thematic study of another culture as part of their reading, writing, viewing and listening activities is *Six Paths to China* (**http://www.kn.pacbell.com/wired/China/index.html**). Californian English language arts teacher Tom March created this site to illustrate to teachers how they might make the best use of the Internet in developing their own websites and hypertextual activities. As its title implies, this site contains six different approaches ("paths") to teaching students via the Internet about contemporary China.

In the first activity, called "China on the Net," March has collected a hotlist of resources from which teachers can derive their own student research projects if they wish. As part of a unit on Chinese and Chinese-American stories, for example, your students could, following March's first path to China, find sites on the arts, the environment, international relations, human rights, and many other topics.

March's second path, "Exploring China," encourages students to create their own multimedia scrapbooks in HTML (HyperText Markup Language) by developing a website of their own. Alternatively, they could employ other hypermedia software modes such as Hyperstudio to create a presentation from downloaded texts, images, videoclips, and audioclips of China's places, cultures, and politics. The third path, "The Treasures of China," involves an Internet-based treasure hunt for information about China's past with which to answer questions about China's present situation, such as "What is China doing in Tibet that disturbs the Dalai Lama?"

In the final three activities March encourages students to examine their own feelings on issues. He asks them to carry out inquiry-based research and to conduct a role-playing activity. Each of his six approaches to studying various aspects of China is based upon a wealth of World Wide Web resources both from within China and from sites around the world.

The special value of the *Six Paths to China* project as a source of English language arts activities lies in its ability to expose students to multimedia representations of China that have been carefully designed by the site's author to help students avoid simplistic, stereotypical conclusions about the Chinese people.

Model 7: Doing Author Studies

As you will see in Chapter 4, there is a vast selection of Internet sites regarding authors for children and adolescents. If your students are reading the works of Judy Blume, for instance, they can visit her home page to learn more about her (**http://www.judyblume.com/menu-main.html**). Blume provides young readers with information about her latest book and lists of other books by her which they might wish to read. She answers their frequently asked questions and provides biographical information and photographs of herself. We learn that Judy is founder and trustee of the Kids Fund, which is supported by royalties from several of her books, including *Letters to Judy,* a book of letters from her young readers. In her *Writing Tips* section she talks about writing "from the inside," keeping a trusty notebook, finding your own style, and rewriting. Judy emphasizes the importance of teachers being supportive of the creative writing attempts of students.

At Virginia Hamilton's home page (http://www.virginiahamilton.com/) the famous children's book writer provides many interesting features, including biographical background information. When she was a young girl she would sit enthralled listening to her mother tell stories that she had herself heard as a child from Virginia's grandfather, about his escape from slavery to Ohio along the Underground Railroad. Descriptions of her books, such as *Her Story,* which contains folk tales, fairy tales, and true tales of African American women, are available, as well as a short interview with Hamilton done by amazon.com. She also includes an informative page about her 1996 visit to South Africa, which contains related links about apartheid and Nelson Mandela. Hamilton encourages her young readers to send her e-mail.

Model 8: Researching Stories from Other Times and Places

This model for using the Internet to teach literature enables your students to make comparisons among a wide variety of cultures through their storytelling traditions. For K–6 students the site titled *Tales of Wonder: Folk and Fairy Tales from Around the World* at (**http://darsie.ucdavis.edu/tales/**) contains a large and truly wonderful collection of tales including stories from countries such as China, England, India, Japan, and Russia as well as links to many more interesting folk and fairy tale sites. Students of all ages can enjoy comparing the themes and characters of these stories from different places. They will also notice, for instance, variations within countries such as the Tamil, Punjabi, Kashmiri, and Bengali cultures from which some of the Indian tales derive. To facilitate your students' understanding of these tales you might also involve them in research on the Internet into the features of the diverse cultures represented on this site.

The literatures represented on the *Multicultural and World Literature for Middle and Secondary Schools* site (**http://falcon.jmu.edu/~ramseyil/worldlit.htm**) are Russian, African, and Latin American. These links have been selected with middle and secondary school students in mind and are all of high quality in terms of the opportunities for hypertextual interaction and multicultural understanding. For instance, one of the links to Latin American literature provides nine excellent and detailed unit plans on *The Modern Short Story* in Latin America. Writers discussed in these units include Gabriel Gracia Marquez and Jorge Luis Borges. Some of the topics include "Mexico's History and Literature," "The Latin American Short Story: A Cultural Tradition," and "Puerto Rico: Its Land, History, Culture, and Literature."

Model 9: Having Fun with Media Literacy

In this model for using the Internet in your language arts program we wish to emphasize the pleasure that you and your students can experience in viewing and listening to media on the Internet and in producing your own video and audio presentations to share with others around the world. A good place to start when looking for worthwhile media literacy lesson plans is the University of Oregon's *Media Literacy Online Project* site (**http://interact.uoregon.edu/MediaLit/HomePage**). Among the topics you will find there are advertising, critical viewing skills, news reporting, photo and visual arts, radio production, web page design, and script writing. One of the many sites to which *The Media Literacy Online Project* (**http://interact.uoregon.edu/MediaLit/HomePage**) is connected through its *Children's Radio and Audio Media* link is the *Warner Brothers' Looney Tunes Karaoke* site were K–6 students can enjoy themselves by singing "Be Kind to Your Web-Footed Friends" with Daffy Duck or "A-Hunting We Will Go" with Elmer Fudd. Or they can learn how to create their own radio shows and share them as audio files with students in other schools by visiting the site titled *How to Make Your Own Radio Program*.

For an excellent source of Canadian news and information shows, your students can visit the site titled *CBC On The Web* at (**www.cbc.ca/main.shtml**). Here they may view transcripts of the television news show, *The National*, dating back to 1996, or they can download archived audio files of the radio progams. Transcripts of *The National* can be searched by date or subject, so if your students are doing research on "First Nations Issues" as part of a "Native Literature" unit and they want to view the text version of all of the news items referring to Aboriginal organizations, they can simply type in the words "First Nations" to find more than 20 items from 1997 and 1998.

Your K–6 students may wish to follow the link from the *CBC On The Web* site to the *CBC 4 Kids* site. Here, for example, children can listen to radio plays written and performed by grade 4 students. Then they can produce their own plays to submit to the CBC. Or they can take a virtual tour of the CBC Sound Effects Studio in Toronto to see how the radio technicians there produce the sounds of trains, the wind, marching feet, prison doors, and more.

In all these models for using the Internet in your teaching, the students can grow in their knowledge of the world and themselves by collaborating on the Internet in reading, writing, speaking, listening, and viewing activities. The teacher in each case assumes the role as facilitator and guide of research and writing projects in which the walls of their classrooms dissolve, the distance between countries collapses, and students learn primarily from one another and from the materials which they find on the Internet. There are many other models for Internet use, some of which you will infer from the rest of this book, but the key point we wish to make here is that you need to rethink your role as a teacher when attempting to find or develop new curriculum approaches that involve the Internet.

ROLE OF THE TEACHER

Technology has greatly influenced the ways teachers teach and students learn. It puts teachers and students into a collaborative research mode. Students often teach themselves because they have in-depth knowledge about a topic as a result of their research via the Internet. This might be threatening to a traditional teacher because the power is shifted to the student. However, the responsibility of constructing knowledge must be rightfully returned to the learner!

With the use of the Internet's resources, teachers can put into practice Howard Gardner's theory of *multiple intelligences* very effectively, thus meeting the needs and interests of students. Students do not have to be locked into space, time, and resources. For example, Updegrove (1995) reports that in the Apple Classrooms of Tomorrow (ACOT) research project, in which high school students had many opportunities to use computers and networks to enhance their learning,

> *Students had significant growth in their independence and their ability to be collaborative problem solvers and communicators. . . . Teachers have shifted their educational approach from one of knowledge transfer (instructionism) to one of knowledge building (constructivism). Classroom instruction shifted from traditional lecture model to one that depended heavily on student collaboration and*

peer teaching (Apple Education Research Series, summary as cited in Updegrove, 1995).

Computers put the students in the ACOT project in contact with resources worldwide. The teacher's responsibility for stimulating students' interest in a subject still remains, which means guiding the students' thinking about a subject and challenging the student to be creative in his or her approach to analyzing the topic at hand. The teacher is a mentor and plays an interactive role with his or her students.

Internet resources allow English teachers to be highly creative in their teaching. Whereas students used to compare their ideas about literature with their peers in the same classroom, now they can share their interpretations of literature with students on the other side of the globe (Greenlaw, 1992).

K–12 READING AND LANGUAGE ARTS SITES

We include in this section a sampling of some of the ready-to-use interactive language arts units that are available for you on the Internet. Simply follow the instructions of the units' authors, and you will experience with your students just how enjoyable the Internet's language arts and reading sites can be.

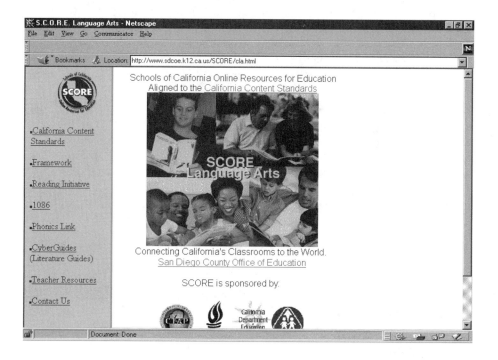

SCORE K–12 English Language Arts Cyber Guides

The Schools of California Online Resources for Education (SCORE) site (**http://www.sdcoe.k12.ca.us/SCORE/cla.html**) is one of the best sources of such units. It contains approximately 140 web-based unit plans for grades K–3, 4–5, 6–8, and 9–12 English language arts teachers to use with their students. To give you a sense of the amazing variety of interactive activities that these units provide we will briefly describe four of them for you. These four units are based on Laura Ingalls Wilder's *Little House in the Big Woods,* Farley Mowat's *Owls in the Family,* Paul Zindel's *The Pigman,* and Aldous Huxley's *Brave New World.*

At the beginning of the grade 3 unit plan for Laura Ingalls Wilder's *Little House in the Big Woods,* students are shown images of cabins in the woods and asked to draw a picture of one of them and to write a description of what they see, using concrete sensory details. Then they are to read a description of wolves taken from the novel and view images of wolves in order to answer the question, "Why is the wolf the bad guy?" In the third activity the students are to read a number of recipes for maple sugar and then to write a maple sugar recipe of their own. The fourth activity involves students visiting an Internet site that features an authentic letter written by Laura Ingalls Wilder. After reading Laura's letter, students write a letter of their own to the children of the future telling them what life is like for a third grader in today's world. Finally, students are encouraged to read book reviews written by other students on the Internet and to then write their own reviews of the novel, *Little House in the Big Woods.*

The approach to teaching Farley Mowat's *Owls in the Family* to grade 4 or 5 students involves first of all guiding the students to sites on the weather and scenery of Saskatoon, Saskatchewan, in order for them to write a comparison between Saskatoon and their own hometown. Next the students are asked to conduct a virtual dissection of an owl pellet to determine what owls like to eat. Then, after visiting sites that contain images of the owl, they draw a picture of one of them. After writing and editing a friendly letter, the students are asked to visit two Farley Mowat author biography sites and to take notes on his life. They are then asked to make a list of things from Farley Mowat's life that appear in the book, *Owls in the Family.*

For Paul Zindel's *The Pigman* the authors of this web unit have included the following activities:

1. First, in order to be able to trace the excursions that John and Lorraine made with Mr. Pignatti, they make a map of New York City based upon five different maps that they are directed to on the Internet.

2. Then they go on virtual visits to sites about the Guggenheim Museum, the Statue of Liberty, and Time Square.

3. Next they see slide shows of baboons and ceramic pigs and write an essay about the significance of these two symbols in the novel.

4. After this they send their teacher an electronic postcard in which they briefly descibe their favorite setting in the story.

5. For the final activity, the students are asked to view a Venn Diagram page to see how they can then create their own diagram to chart the similarities and differences among John, Lorraine, and Mr. Pignatti in three overlapping circles.

The five activities associated with Aldous Huxley's *Brave New World* involve students in writing four short essays and creating one simulation game by visiting pertinent sites on the Internet and doing research. The first essay, for instance, is on brainwashing, so the students carry out their reseach at sites on propaganda and advertising techniques. The other three essays deal with issues of cloning, legal constraints on people's freedom, and various social problems such as class warfare, mass culture, genetic ethics, and the dangers of Prozac. In the multimedia simulation activity, by using a free, downloadable multimedia authoring tool called Cocoa, the students create a world that illustrates the concept of conformity.

From this brief survey of just four of the many wonderful unit plans available at these language arts cyber guide sites, we hope that you now have a sense of the potential not only to make use of SCORE's teaching activities but also of how you might develop some of your own cyber guides in the future.

Doucette Index K–12 Literature-Based Teaching Ideas

http://www.educ.ucalgary.ca/litindex/

The Doucette Index of literature-based teaching ideas is a tremendous site, especially for teachers who are looking for print resources about commonly taught works of literature. The site contains a search engine that asks you to type in the title and/or author of a book you wish to teach. If, for example, you enter the title *Julius Caesar* into the search engine, you will find a list of five excellent, web-based teaching resources on the play and another six print-based teaching resources.

Blue Web'n: Blue Ribbon Learning Sites on the Web

The Blue Web'n page **http://www.kn.pacbell.com/wired/bluewebn/index.html** provides links to Internet sites containing (at the time of this writing) 4 tutorials, 45 activities, 8 projects, 23 lessons, 25 hotlists, 111 resources, and 15 references and tools for use by K–12 English language arts teachers and students. Here is a brief sampling of some of the descriptions of the valuable resources you will find at the Blue Web'n site.

Tutorials

■ *Writing Argumentative Essays.* Bill Daly, of the Victoria University of Technology (Australia), has provided a service to new writing teachers, high school students, and parents trying to help their children piece together an effective argumentative essay.

■ *The Shiki Haiku Salon.* This tutorial provides resources and a lesson in the poetic form of the haiku.

Activities

■ *Seussville.* These simple Shockwave games are fun activities for young children based on the popular Dr. Seuss books.

■ *Cyber English Syllaweb.* Here are some online English assignments that use technologies as tools and topics. The site, created by English teacher Ted Nellen, includes a booklist of literature with technology themes.

Projects

■ *Project Bartleby (Columbia University).* This is the home of great literary websites on such people as Emily Dickinson, W. E. B. Du Bois, Robert Frost, John Keats, Herman Melville, Edna St. Vincent Millay, and Gertrude Stein. The site includes full text of writings by these authors.

▪ *Children's Express.* This is a news service produced by kids reporting on the issues that affect their lives.

Lessons

▪ *Deep in the Bush, Where People Rarely Ever Go.* According to the Blue Web'n description of this site, the stories used in this lesson were collected by teacher Phillip Martin while serving as a Peace Corps volunteer in Liberia, West Africa. Included at this site is an extensive teacher lesson page, African recipes, links to other African resources, and ideas for your students to create and produce their own plays.

▪ *The Jurassic Park Interdisciplinary Activities Page.* This interdisciplinary unit includes activities for students to do after viewing Steven Spielberg's film, *Jurassic Park.* Students are invited to send e-mail, poetry, essays, and artwork.

Hotlists

▪ *Webtime Stories.* Replacing the *Kiddie Lit on the Net* site, this is an annotated hotlist of exceptional online stories, book and author resources, and online activites for people who love children's literature.

▪ *Great Books Interdisciplinary Matrix.* Intended to support study of the "Great Books" championed by Mortimer Adler and Charles Van Doren, this site provides links to resources on 150 authors, many from the reading list for "How to Read a Book."

Resources

▪ *Midlink Magazine.* This is an electronic magazine for students in the middle grades. Classes are invited to participate in a variety of online projects and activities.

▪ *The Internet Classics Archive.* This site features 441 works of classical literature by 59 authors, including Aesop, Aeschylus, Homer, Ovid, and Plato. Visitors can read classic works, in their entirety, participate in discussions of the works, and bone up on the authors themselves.

References and Tools

▪ *Visual Thesaurus.* In this interesting way of exploring English language synonyms, words show up as a "spatial map of linguistic associations," with clickable words that encourage you to follow threads. The site uses *Java* and works best on newer systems.

■ *Biography.* A&E's Biography website includes a searchable and browsable online collection of 15,000 cross-referenced biographies from the Cambridge Biographical Encyclopedia. The site also provides selected opening chapters and reviews from best-selling biographies, a quiz, anagram game, chatboards, and schedules of upcoming episodes of the *Biography* television program.

SUGGESTED ACTIVITIES

1. Using e-mail, contact teachers in two other schools. They can be teachers you know already in schools close to your own or teachers in schools in other states or countries. Arrange to have your students collaborate via e-mail in the writing of a group short story, novel, or poetry anthology.

2. Using e-mail, contact teachers in another country and plan to have your students collaborate with theirs in the interpretation of short stories, poems, novels, or plays. (Hint: It may be easiest to find common reading materials to study if you choose texts available on the Internet.)

3. Using e-mail, contact either some professional writers or, in the case of younger students, some senior citizens who might be willing to act as readers and editors of the creative writing your students produce. These mentoring relationships require some effort to set up, but they can be extremely rewarding for all involved.

4. With the help of parent volunteers, take your students out into the community with cameras and tape recorders with specific research plans in mind. Have them conduct interviews in order to paint a picture of your community on your school's home page. The end result should help visitors to your school's website understand your community and it should also engender a sense of place and pride in your students.

5. Visit several school field trip sites such as the one described in Model 5. Once you have a clear idea of how you would like to create a similar site yourself, take your students on a field trip and then, through your school's home page, share the experience with the world. An interesting variation of this activity involves taking your students on a virtual field trip and then having them compose a multimedia presentation of the experience on the Internet. They might, for instance, take the field trip to Mars (the actual or imagined planet), to Shakespeare's England, or to Jurassic Park.

6. After studying Tom March's *Six Paths to China,* involve your students in creating their own "Six Paths" to India, Brazil, or Italy.

7. Have each of your students visit a website devoted to one of their favorite authors. Each student should be responsible for researching a different author, but all of the authors can be writing in a particular genre (humor, adventure, science fiction, etc.) if you wish. After they have studied the site and read one of the authors' books, they can present a book talk and short author biography to the class.

8. Take your students to the *Tales of Wonder* or the *Multicultural and World Literature* site and have them carry out comparisons of two stories from different countries in order to discover common themes and archetypal patterns. Then encourage the students to write a similar tale set in their own culture. They may need to do further research on the Internet to learn more about the cultural backgrounds of each of the stories they are to interpret.

9. With your students, visit some of the many multimedia sites such as the *Looney Tunes Karioke* page on the Internet and enjoy with them the activities available. If, for instance, you visit the *CBC 4 Kids* site, you could learn with the students how radio technicians generate various sound effects, then have the students create their own sound effects and write and record radio plays making use of these sounds.

10. Visit a number of the language arts interactive web units at the SCORE and Blue Web'n sites that are intended for students in the grade level(s) you teach. Select one of these units to share with your students.

SUMMARY

Clearly, a new paradigm for the teaching of reading and English language arts is emerging in which you need to be able to facilitate your students' learning on the Internet. Although the the list of nine models for Internet use provided in this chapter is certainly not an exhaustive one, we hope that it has provided you with a sense of the possibilities that await you as you begin to consider your new role as a guide on the Information Superhighway.

REFERENCES

Cummins, J. and Sayers, D. (1995). *Brave new schools: Challenging cultural illiteracy through global learning networks.* New York: St. Martin's Press.

Greenlaw, J. C. (1992). Reading between worlds: Computer-mediated intercultural responses to Asian literature. *Reader: Essays in Reader-Oriented Theory, Criticism, and Pedagogy,* 28, 37–51.

Landow, G. (1997). *Hypertext 2.0: The convergence of contemporary critical theory and technology.* Baltimore: The Johns Hopkins Press.

Mori, Y. (1991). Spring storm. In S. Jeroski (Ed.), *Tapestries: Short stories from the Pacific Rim.* Scarborough, Ontario: Nelson Canada.

O'Neil, J. (1995). Technology and schools: A conversation with Chris Dede. *Educational Leadership,* October, 7–12.

Updegrove, K. H. (1995). *Teaching on the Internet.* **http://pobox.upenn.edu/~kimu/teaching.html**

CHAPTER 3

Reading Research and Lessons

- Teaching Reading

- Whole Language and Phonics

- Enabling Readers to Overcome Reading Disabilities

- Reading Recovery

- Gifted Readers

- Fun with Words

- Storytime

- Lesson Plans for Teaching Reading

- Reading Across the Curriculum

TEACHING READING

Do you occasionally feel overwhelmed when you are faced with the task of teaching 30 students how to read? In a single class you may need to instruct children who are reading at various grade levels, some who are challenged by learning disabilities, and others who are gifted readers. You have been told by parents, principals, and professors that you must become aware of the many theories and methods of reading, such as whole language, reading recovery, and reading across the curriculum, but when you set out to make sense of these different pedagogical approaches, you discover that the field contains multiple, conflicting schools of thought. As will become clear in this chapter, the Internet can serve as a valuable resource for your work as a teacher of reading, whether your students are preschoolers or adults. In the following pages you will encounter brief summaries of articles and sites on the Internet that provide information about a wide range of issues and approaches from the field of reading research. You will also find a wonderful selection of reading lessons, enjoyable vocabulary activities, and storybooks on the web with which to entice your students into a lifetime of reading pleasure.

Learning to Read

http://toread.com/

The first site, titled *Learning to Read*, is the best place to start. The author, John Nemes, provides a clearly organized and comprehensive account of the reading

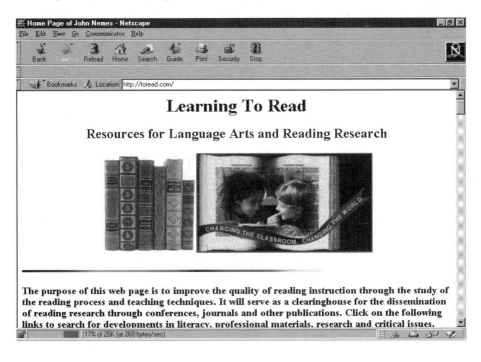

process. He explains that there are basically three models of reading: (1) the *top-down models,* emphasizing what the reader brings to the text, such as prior knowledge and experiences; (2) the *bottom-up models,* emphasizing the written or printed text based on the idea that comprehension begins by processing the smallest linguistic unit (phonemes) first and then working toward the larger units (words, phrases, sentences); and (3) the *integrated models,* which recognize the interaction of bottom-up and top-down processes simultaneously throughout the reading process.

Among the topics discussed at the Learning to Read site are Using Cues for Reading Activities for Teaching Reading, What Are Literature Circles?, The Value of Free Reading, Book Discussions, Facts on the Teaching of Phonics, What Are Reading Skills?, Scaffolding and Modeling Strategies, Reading Comprehension Strategies, Teaching Word Identification, and Facts on Teaching Skills in Context. This site also contains an excellent collection of links to professional organizations, publications, authors, publishers, and interactive lessons. One of the many delightful interactive lessons, for instance, is a very rich unit for grade 1 children called *Teddybears.* This includes objectives, outcomes, activities, background information on teddybears, stories, poems, assessment strategies, and lists of related books, videos and websites. The *Teddybear* unit has the potential to enchant beginning readers for many weeks.

After you have visited the Learning to Read site, you may wish to study some of the topics mentioned there in greater depth by examining the full text of the following reading research articles and books on the Internet.

Beginning Reading Instruction

http://www.just4kids.org/html/bri.html

Beginning Reading Instruction is an online publication of the Texas Education Agency. Mike Moses, Commissioner of Education for Texas, explains that this article is intended to address the problem of an ever growing population of children coming to school who have barely even seen a book, much less had the thousands of hours of lap reading, vocabulary building, and positive experiences with letters and sounds that are so essential to learning to read. Thus 12 essential components of research-based programs for beginning reading instruction are detailed. Among these components are that children have opportunities to expand their use and appreciation of oral and printed language, hear good stories and informational books read aloud daily, understand and manipulate the building blocks of spoken and written language, learn the relationship between the sounds of spoken language and the letters of written language, practice accurate and fluent reading of decodable stories, read and comprehend a wide assortment of books and other texts, develop and comprehend new vocabulary through wide reading and direct vocabulary instruction, and apply comprehension strategies as they reflect upon and think critically about what they read. In addition, eight features of classrooms that support effective beginning reading instruction are listed, including encouraging children to read widely and engaging them in classroom discussions about the books they have read.

Seven Promising Programs for Reading and English Language Arts

http://www.aft.org/edissues/whatworks/seven/index.htm

The American Federation of Teachers has provided an extensive description of several exemplary reading programs: *Seven Promising Programs for Reading and English Languages Arts.* The programs were selected according to whether they were designed to (1) help all students acquire the skills and/or knowledge they need to successfully perform to high academic standards; (2) had proved effective in raising the academic achievement levels of "at-risk" students in low-performing schools based on independent evaluations; (3) had been effectively implemented in multiple sites beyond the original pilot school(s); and (4) offered professional development, materials, and ongoing implementation support, either through the program's developer, independent contractors, or dissemination networks established by schools already in the program. The seven programs chosen are Cooperative Integrated Reading and Comprehension (CIRC), Direct Instruction, Exemplary Center for Reading Instruction (ECRI), Junior Great Books (JGB), Multicultural Reading and Thinking (McRAT), Open Court Collections for Young Scholars (OC), and Success for All (SFA).

The Multicultural Reading and Thinking (McRAT) program, for example, was developed in the mid-1980s by the Arkansas Department of Education in conjunction with reading specialists and classroom teachers for use with students at all achievement levels. It is a supplementary program, designed to improve students' reading, writing, and thinking skills by teaching them to read reflectively, develop and supply evidence for their opinions, and communicate ideas effectively in writing. Teachers are trained to infuse culturally diverse themes and materials into existing curricula and to develop critical reading and thinking skills in students that can be used across subject areas and in daily life.

Stony Brook Reading and Language Project

http://www.read+lang.sbs.sunysb.edu/

Grover Whitehurst provides this introductory page for the *Stony Brook Reading and Language Project.* From it, you can proceed to pages on the project itself, or a list of papers and publications, many of which are available in full text. In one of their more recent online articles, *Outcomes of an Emergent Literacy Intervention from Head Start through Second Grade,* for instance, Whitehurst and his colleagues state that although children in the sample began formal reading instruction with relatively low levels of emergent literacy skills, they showed substantial gains with respect to national norms by the end of second grade. Addressing the nature and quality of children's educational environments in the first years of elementary school, they conclude, is likely to be a critical part of the process of generating a nation of readers.

Learning to Read in Culturally Responsive Computer Environments

http://www.ciera.org/products/3rdquarterreports/1-004.pdf

A 30-page monograph, *Learning to Read in Culturally Responsive Environments,* is published by the Center for the Improvement of Early Reading Achievement (CIERA) in *PDF* format, so you can read it in your Netscape browser on Acrobat Reader. Nichole Pinkard from the University of Michigan describes and evaluates two computer-based learning environments: Rappin' Reader and Say Say Oh Playmate. These two environments build upon the lived literacy experiences that African-American children bring to classrooms as scaffolds for early literacy instruction. When Rappin' Reader and Say Say Oh Playmate were used with low-socioeconomic-status African Americans in grades 1–4 attending after-school tutoring/mentoring programs, students made substantial gains on literacy measures such as sight-word knowledge. Pinkard's results suggest at least modest benefits from using culturally responsive reading materials and a computer-based learning environment in literacy instruction.

WHOLE LANGUAGE AND PHONICS

The Whole Language Umbrella

http://www.ncte.org/wlu/about.shtml

The *Whole Language Umbrella* site, provided by the National Council of Teachers of English (NCTE), contains many helpful features for teachers interested in adopting the whole-language approach to teaching reading. For instance, it provides the following list of beliefs shared by whole-language educators:

1. Holistic approach to the acquisition and development of literacy in all its aspects.
2. Positive view of all human learners.
3. Belief that language is central to human learning.
4. Belief that learning is easiest when it is from whole to part, when it is in authentic contexts, and when it is functional for the learners.
5. Belief in the empowerment of learners and teachers.
6. Belief that learning is both personal and social and that classrooms and other educational settings must be learning communities.
7. Acceptance of all learners and the languages, cultures, and experiences they bring to their education.
8. Belief that learning is both joyous and fulfilling.
9. Belief in the developmental nature of learning, which builds on learners' prior knowledge and experience.

Some other useful aspects of this site are its lists of resources, such as Interest/Action Groups, Suggested Readings, Web Sites, Discussion Lists, and Fact Sheets on Whole Language. The Whole Language Umbrella also provides you with information about upcoming literacy conferences and the opportunity to take part in an online discussion forum with other whole-language teachers.

The Reading Wars

http://www.theatlantic.com/issues/97nov/read.htm

Nicholas Lemann, the national correspondent for *The Atlantic Monthly* magazine, explores the political complexities of the battle between advocates of the whole-language and the phonics approaches to teaching reading. In his very entertaining and highly readable article, Lehmann concludes that "given that the traditional side is now winning the ongoing battle between traditional and progressive education, schools all over the country will be pressed hard by parents and politicians to move toward imparting skills and away from simply inculcating the joy of learning."

Sensationalism , Politics, and Literacy: What's Going On?

http://www.pdkintl.org/kappan/kfli9712.htm

In this PDK online article, Rona Flippo provides evidence that despite extreme differences in philosophy, expert reading researchers do agree on a number of practices and contexts with regard to reading instruction and development. These must not be ignored, she warns, in favor of what the politicians think.

Sixty Years of Reading Research—But Who's Listening?

http://www.pdkintl.org/kappan/kzem9903.htm

In another PDK online article, Steve Zemelman, Harvey Daniels, and Marilyn Bizar point out that 60 years of research and thousands of studies that resoundingly validate progressive approaches to literacy learning still have failed to produced the strong consensus we might expect. The authors explain why.

Whole Language and Phonics: Can They Work Together?

http://www.education-world.com/a_curr/curr029.shtml

In her *Education World* article, Sharon Cromwell argues that the majority of experts now contend that neither the whole-language nor the phonics approach by itself is effective all the time, but that both approaches possess merit. What does succeed then, many experts say, is a carefully designed reading program that employs part whole-language approach and part phonics, while taking into account each student's learning style and demonstrated strengths and weaknesses.

ENABLING READERS TO OVERCOME READING DISABILITIES

The Big "R"—Reading

http://www.ldonline.org/ld_indepth/reading/tutor_tips.html

This article offers some sobering facts about why good reading instruction is important. Up to 15 percent of children with reading problems drop out of school; only 2 percent finish college. Approximately 50 percent of teens and young adults with criminal records do not read well. About 50 percent of young people with substance abuse problems do not read well. About 90–95 percent of reading problems can be corrected with early intervention and appropriate instruction.

The following general advice is offered for reading teachers: When it comes to reading, directed practice makes perfect. Never force a child to read orally in front of peers. Choose reading material on subjects of interest to the child. Speak distinctly and expressively when reading, clearly enunciating words and sounds. Inflect your voice in accordance with punctuation. Help make reading enjoyable. Children with reading difficulties usually do not like to read and do not get sufficient practice to become fluent.

The remainder of the article provides valuable strategies for teaching students with reading disablilies such as dyslexia, speech and language disorders, processing deficits, and attention deficit/hyperactivity disorder (ADHD).

Academic Interventions for Children with Dyslexia

http://www.kidsource.com/kidsource/content2/dyslexia.html

This article, written by Julia Frost and Michael Emery for *KidSource Online*, suggests many types of interventions to help dyslexic children to learn to read. Here are just a few of them: Discuss the specific purposes and goals of each reading lesson. Teach children how metacognitive skills should be applied. Provide regular practice with reading materials that are contextually meaningful. Include many words that children can decode. Using books that contain many words children cannot decode may lead to frustration and guessing, which is counterproductive. Teach for automaticity. As basic decoding skills are mastered, regularly expose children to decodable words so that these words become automatically accessible. As a core sight vocabulary is acquired, expose children to more irregular words to increase reading accuracy. Reading-while-listening and repeated reading are useful techniques for developing fluency. Teach for comprehension. Try introducing conceptually important vocabulary prior to initial reading and have children retell the story and answer questions regarding implicit and explicit content.

Preventing Reading Difficulties in Young Children

http://www.nap.edu/readingroom/books/prdyc/

This highly acclaimed study synthesizes the research on early reading development and makes practical, commonsense recommendations. The full 400-page text, edited by Catherine E. Snow, M. Susan Burns, and Peg Griffin for the National Research Council, is available here in HTML format. The study provides recommendations under the following headings: Literacy Instruction in First Through Third Grades, Promoting Literacy Development in Preschool and Kindergarten, Education and Professional Development for All Involved in Literacy Instruction, Teaching Reading to Speakers of Other Languages, Ensuring Adequate Resources to Meet Children's Needs, and Addressing the Needs of Children with Persistent Reading Difficulties.

Helping Children Overcome Reading Difficulties

http://www.indiana.edu/~eric_rec/ieo/digests/d72.html

This Digest #72 from the *ERIC Clearinghouse on Reading, English, and Communication* provides teachers who are looking for a factual, research-based summary of current knowledge on reading difficulties with some excellent suggestions on how to help their students to overcome the problems of dyslexia.

READING RECOVERY

Reading Recovery

http://www.indiana.edu/~eric_rec/ieo/digests/d106.html

In this *ERIC Clearinghouse on Reading, English, and Communication* Digest #106, reading recovery is described as a system of intense one-on-one assistance for students with reading difficulties, adapted from practices pioneered in New Zealand. It has been gaining popularity in the United States. The digest's author, Roger Sensenbaugh, describes the program and some of the research dealing with it, and offers suggestions for further reading.

Reading Recovery Council of North America

http://www.readingrecovery.org/

The website provided by the Reading Recovery Council of North America describes reading recovery as an early intervention designed to help children who are at the lowest levels of achievement in reading and writing to become proficient readers and writers. Reading recovery assists first-grade children in catching up with their

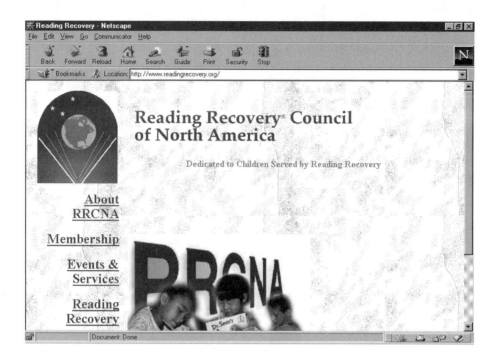

peers. The articles in this website are intended to provide basic information about reading recovery, to report on a variety of research and evaluation studies, and to provide access to articles that may be of interest to visitors to the site.

GIFTED READERS

Gifted Readers and Reading Instruction

http://www.indiana.edu/~eric_rec/ieo/digests/d101.html

In reviewing for *ERIC* the professional literature on reading instruction for gifted readers, Norma Decker Collins and Nola Kortner Aiex have identified several salient points about gifted readers:

1. Gifted readers usually master basic reading skills by the time they come to school and are ready for complex concepts at an early age.

2. Gifted readers tend to have an internal locus of control—they believe that achievement is the result of their own ability and behavior.

3. Gifted readers need instruction in reading that is different from a regular class-room program.

4. Instruction for very able readers should focus on developing higher cognitive-level comprehension skills.

5. Teaching reading to gifted readers requires more than a skills-oriented approach.

6. Books for gifted readers should be selected on the basis of quality language—books that use varied and complex language structures are a primary source of cognitive growth.

7. Reading programs for gifted readers should foster a desire to read.

8. A reading program for gifted readers should include a variety of reading materials and strategies that are based on the present needs and demands of the reader, not on the chronological age or grade level.

FUN WITH WORDS

Word Play

http://www.wolinskyweb.com/word.htm

This incredible site contains a list of links to more than 150 other sites where your students can have fun with words. Here are just five of the delightful activities that await K–12 students:

1. *American Slanguages:* Choose a city and learn to talk like the locals.

2. *Brain Food:* Give your mind a workout with this devious collection of puzzles. There are hundreds, ranging from word games to logic problems to riddles. Some are tricky. Some require innovation. All require thinking power.

3. *Create Your Own Shakespearean Insults:* Combine one word from each of three columns, preface with "Thou"—and thus shalt thou have the perfect insult. Let thyself go—mix and match to find a barb worthy of the Bard.

4. *Hangman:* Interactive game where you have to figure out the letters in a word before the stick figure swings.

5. *Little Explorers:* A multilingual (English; English-Spanish; English-French) picture dictionary with wonderful graphics and links.

AltaVista Translation Service

http://babelfish.altavista.digital.com/cgi-bin/translate?

In this amazing translation site you write or cut and paste text into the space provided, and within seconds it is translated from English into French, Spanish, Portuguese, German, or Italian, or vice versa. For real fun, try translating something into a second language and then back again into the original language.

STORYTIME

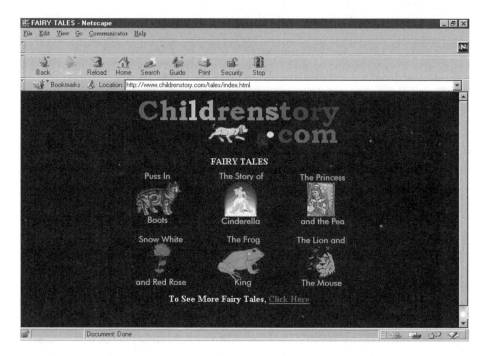

Childrenstory.com

http://www.childrenstory.com/tales/index.html

Here is a collection of many of the most popular fairy tales such as "Sleeping Beauty" and "Snow White."

Heroes

http://www.mythweb.com/heroes/heroes.html

In this collection of ancient tales about Jason, Hercules, Odysseus, and others, the stories are illustrated with comical cartoon drawings that are certain to delight your students.

Mayan Folktales

http://www.folkart.com/~latitude/folktale/folktale.htm

Fernando Penalosa is a retired sociolinguist who most recently taught sociology, linguistics, and Chicano studies at California State University, Long Beach. For over 12 years he has been working with Maya in Guatemala and the Los Angeles area, studying their languages and oral literature. On this site he presents his translations of the following Mayan tales: The Disobedient Son, A Mayan Life, The Rabbit and the Coyote, The Rabbit Throws Out His Sandal, and The Jaguar and the Little Skunk.

Native American Lore Index Page

http://www.ilhawaii.net/~stony/loreindx.html

This site contains more than 130 different Native American tales by Blackfoot, Mic-Mac, Cherokee, Hopi, Cheyenne, Iroquois, and many other First Nations storytellers.

Books Every Child Should Read

http://homearts.com/depts/relat/bookintr.htm

This site contains a series of interviews with people ranging from Captain Kangaroo and Maurice Sendak to Harold Bloom and Maya Angelou, all recommending titles and offering advice on encouraging children to read.

Children's Literature Reference Resources: An Annotated Bibliography

http://www.lib.wmc.edu/pub/bibs/haffner.html

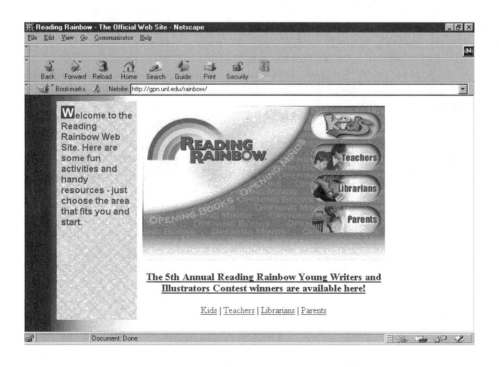

If you are unsure how to locate suitable reading material for children or young adults, take a look at Penny Haffner's guide to print and Internet bibliographies and selection tools.

Reading Rainbow
http://gpn.unl.edu/rainbow/

At this site students and teachers can learn more about the books that are featured on the popular *Reading Rainbow* television show. For instance, information on Episode 21 concerning the book *Paul Bunyan* by author/illustrator Steven Kellogg includes several Internet links to sites where students and teachers can learn more about Arbor Day. Also, there are lists of supplemental books such as *The Bunyans* for children who want to read more about this legendary hero of New England.

Bedtime Stories
http://the-office.com/bedtime-story/

This award-winning site contains wonderfully illustrated web versions of many fine children's stories. The illustrations for *Alice In Wonderland*, for example, are both stunningly beautiful and humorous.

Read *Write* Now!
http://www.parentsplace.com/readroom/education/rwnintro.html

This series of activities for reading and writing fun has been developed for use with children from birth to grade 6. Adapted from the U.S. Department of Education publications, the pages include advice, activities, and suggestions for further reading.

Recommended Youth Reading
http://www.st-charles.lib.il.us/low/ythread.htm

The St. Charles (IL) Public Library's Youth Services Division has compiled this set of 42 bibliographies on diverse topics such as sports, science fiction, and ghost stories, as well as books to help children cope with divorce, moving, the new baby, and child safety. There are also "read-alikes" for popular titles such as *Titanic Crossing*. Some of the lists are annotated.

LESSON PLANS FOR TEACHING READING

Internet Public Library Reading Zone—Picture Books

http://www.ipl.org/cgi-bin/youth/youth.out.pl?sub=rzn2000

This site contains many fine, contemporary, illustrated stories for children. For instance, *The Adventures of Shakey Snake,* written by Patricia Whidden and illustrated by Jennifer Whidden, is a splendidly funny story about a gentle, curious, sometimes sneaky—but always amusing—little rattlesnake. If children wish to, they can write e-mail to Shakey or they can print pictures from the Shakey coloring book.

Sample Book Ideas for Literature-Based Reading Enthusiasts

http://www.acs.ucalgary.ca/~dkbrown/yrca_samp.html

Gale Sherman and Bette Ammon provide extensive lesson plans for several popular, award-winning novels for children and young adults. Their ideas for books such as Avi's *Who Was That Masked Man, Anyway?* include reviews of the book, a list of the awards it has won, information about the author, a plot summary, reading-aloud and book-talk suggestions, activities for drama, language arts, radio plays, and creative writing, as well as lists of other books by Avi that the students might like to read.

Scavenger Hunts

http://www.occdsb.on.ca/~red/htm/scaven.htm

As the authors of this site point out, their web-based scavenger hunts can easily be integrated into your curriculum. Their goal is to provide computer-based, independent Internet activities for a range of grade levels and abilities. You will find that they are based on elementary curriculum themes while incorporating the basics of Internet navigation. The Egyptian Mystery scavenger hunt, for example, is intended for grade 4–6 students. It contains a wonderful set of questions and activities for the children to work on while they explore on their own various Internet sites on pyramids, mummies, and hieroglyphs.

Teachers.Net Reading.

http://www.teachers.net/cgi-bin/lessons/sort.cgi?searchterm=Reading

The *Teachers.Net Reading* site contains more than 150 lessons posted by participating teachers. For example, Dr. Candy Carlile's elementary Reading lesson titled *Sight Word Soup* involves students in memorizing 10 new commonly used words each week by playing various games such as Bingo and Go Fish with them. The students then learn how to read the words in a sentence.

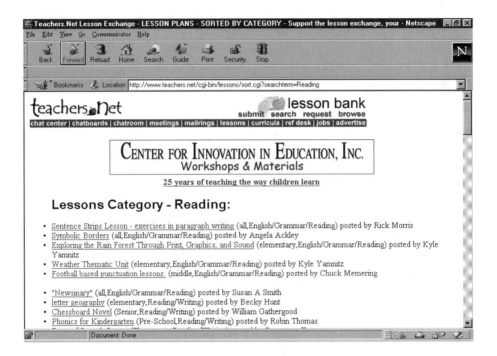

SimonSaysKids.Com Teacher's Lounge Language Arts Lesson Plans

http://www.simonsays.com/kids/teachers/index.cfm

The SimonSaysKids.Com site contains background information and discussion questions about popular mystery and science fiction novels such as the R.L. Stine books and the Star Trek series. There are more than 50 of these lesson plans available at this site.

READING ACROSS THE CURRICULUM

http://www.scholastic.com/instructor/curriculum/index.htm#langarts

Scholastic's *Across the Curriculum: Language Arts* site contains several powerfully written online articles by leading writers in the field of reading research. For instance, Lucy Calkins, well-known as director of the Teachers College Reading Project, has contributed an article titled *Get Real About Reading*, and Dorothy Strickland, who has served as president of the International Reading Association, has written an article titled *Balanced Literacy:Teaching the Skills AND Thrills of Reading.*

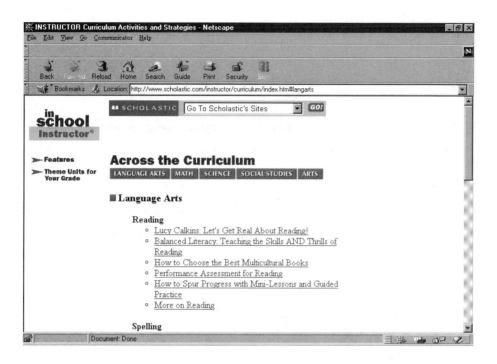

Improving Student Understanding of Textbook Content

**http://www.ldonline.org/ld_indepth/teaching_techniques/
understanding_textbooks.html**

This online article's textbook teaching and learning model is based on cognitive learning theory. It offers educators a new set of practices to show students how they may best learn the new content in three phases: before reading, during reading, and after reading. The article's author, Barbara Flanagan, offers a brief synopsis of the three phases and some teaching suggestions for each phase.

SUGGESTED ACTIVITIES

1. After reading some of the research articles in the first section of this chapter about learning to read, make a list of the additional strategies and beginning reading lessons you want to add to your own set of reading pedagogies. Then discuss your newly discovered theories and lesson plans with other reading teachers in your school. Of the seven promising reading programs examined by the American Federation of Teachers, which program do you think would best suit the needs of your students?

2. In the section of this chapter devoted to the never ending battle between proponents of whole language and phonics there are several compelling arguments. Where do you situate yourself in this debate, and what have you learned from

these articles that will help you to defend your position when asking your principal for more teaching materials in the future?

3. From the research on reading disabilities mentioned in this chapter, develop a set of strategies that you intend to try with your dyslexic and ADHD students the next time you teach them reading.

4. Examine the sites and articles on reading recovery and gifted readers, and compare the approaches taken to these two groups of students in our schools. Then plan how you can accommodate both sets of students in your classroom at the same time.

5. Take a day with your students to play with some of the many fun-with-words sites mentioned in this chapter. For instance, you could have your students use the Altavista translator to write e-mail messages to students in France, Germany, and Mexico. Or you could use it to help them translate poems from French or Spanish into English.

6. Take your elementary students to visit one of the many story sites mentioned in this chapter, and encourage them to each select a different story to retell to the class. Where possible, enable the students to use the illustrations to help them remember how their selected story goes.

7. Choose a dozen lesson plans from the reading lesson plan sites discussed in this chapter, and use them as the foundation for preparing a theme unit to teach to your class.

8. After reading the articles by Lucy Calkins, Dorothy Strickland, and Barbara Flanagan on the reading-across-the-curriculum approach, prepare some pre-reading, during-reading, and post-reading activities to guide your students through their study of a nonfiction text.

SUMMARY

Given the volume of research in the area of reading, it is difficult to remain informed about the latest changes in the field. That is why it is reassuring to find articles and monographs by respected writers in reading research such as Lucy Calkins, Dorothy Strickland, and the many other fine reading specialists whose works we have reviewed in this chapter. Similarly, given the often isolated nature of our work as reading teachers, it is good to know that we can enter discussion groups on the Internet through organizations such as the NCTE's Whole Language Umbrella to share our concerns and suggestions with colleagues around the globe. Finally, once we have gained some confidence in our theories about teaching learning-disabled and gifted readers, it is truly exciting to realize that sites such as Childrenstory.com are available to provide us with literature that is a pleasure to teach to these young scholars.

CHAPTER 4

Literature for Children and Adolescents

- Children's Literature
- Young Adult Literature
- Mythology
- Poetry
- Short Stories and Novels
- Drama
- British, American, and Canadian Authors
- Multicultural and World Literature Authors

CHILDREN'S LITERATURE

When you were a child reading or viewing *The Wizard of Oz*, did you ever wonder about tornado warning signs or about what to do if you were caught in a tornado? In this chapter you will not only have those questions answered for you, but you will also be able to consider geographical, artistic, and historical topics associated with Frank Baum's writings. Opportunities on the Internet abound for intertextually linking ideas, sounds, and images to the literature we love to read and teach. Thus, in this chapter, which contains a large collection of literature sites that are in turn linked to thousands of other sites, we hope to make the point that interdisciplinary learning is now easier than ever to achieve with your students through the magic of hypertextuality.

Another way in which the intertextual nature of the Internet may enhance your teaching can be found in the amazing links that are made across and within cultures, whether these connections are made among various children's stories around the world or among the different versions of a single story such as Snow White.

Several fine, comprehensive sites are discussed in this chapter, such as *The Children's Literature Web* Guide and the *Dramatic Exchange*. Through these sites you can find your way to thousands of works of literature. We present here as well sites containing students' creative writing and responses to literature. And you will find in this chapter sites devoted to many of your favorite authors of children's and young adult literature, as well as web pages devoted to the classic writers taught in secondary schools, such as John Steinbeck and William Shakespeare.

Through the mythology sites listed here, your students can explore the similarities among heroes in Greek, Norse, Chinese, and Iroquois tales. Or they can create their own legendary monsters after reading about the werewolves and goblins described in these sites.

After studying haiku written by Japanese poets and by children around the world, your students can write their own poems and post them on the Internet. If you are at a loss for ideas about teaching poetry or for examples of good poetry, sites such as the *Glossary of Poetic Terms* and *Twentieth-century Poetry in English* will help you find what you need.

As you read this chapter, therefore, we suggest that you consider how best to make use of the resources here to involve your students in making their own connections across disciplines and cultures. In the first section, for instance, as you study the various children's literature sites we have selected, ask yourself how your students might be able to better appreciate the work of authors such as Hans Christian Andersen, Beverly Cleary, and Roald Dahl by following some of the links in the sites devoted to their work. In the case of Dahl's site, for example, how might your students come to appreciate his stories better by taking part in the activities recommended by the teachers who have contributed their ideas to the site?

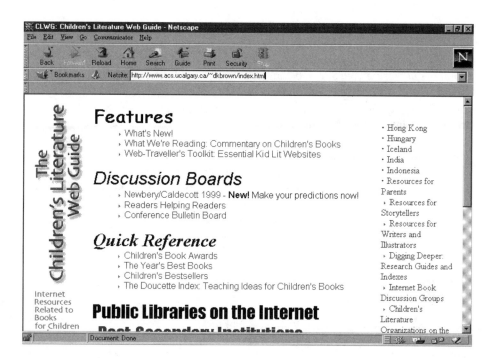

The Children's Literature Web Guide

http://www.acs.ucalgary.ca/~dkbrown/index.html	
Intended Audience	Teachers and students
Grade Level	K-12
Curricular Fit	Children's and young adult literature
Types of Resources	Biographical information on authors, lesson plans, book lists
Authorship of Site	David K. Brown at the University of Calgary
Navigation	Good
Visual Appeal	Good
Interactive Activity	Some opportunity for teachers and students to review books

The *Children's Literature Web Guide* is an excellent place to start your search for children's and young adult literature resources and links. This comprehensive site contains teaching resources such as lesson plans for some books, biographical information about authors, lists of award-winning and best-selling books, a conference bulletin board, journals, book reviews, discussion groups, research guides, children's literature organizations, children's publishers, and book sellers. This site also provides links to many other valuable children's literature sites such as Carol Hurst's *Children's Literature Web Site,* Kay Vandergrift's *Special Interest Page,* and *OzKidz Literature.* If you would like to learn how to write or illustrate children's literature yourself, try the link to *The Purple Crayon,* where you can read advice from children's book editor Harold Underdown.

The next two sites also provide good general lists of information from which you can look for specific details about authors. After describing these two sites we provide a sampling of 15 other web pages about particular writers or genres of children's literature. Most of these sites are of more use to you than to your students. They enable you to learn about the lives and works of famous children's book writers such as Judy Blume and L. M. Montgomery. But some, as we shall point out, are written with your students in mind and are very interactive.

Sites for Children: Literature and Language

http://www.ala.org/parentspage/greatsites/lit.html	
Intended Audience	Teachers
Grade Level	K-8
Curricular Fit	Children's literature
Types of Resources	Lists of links about favorite children's stories, authors
Authorship of Site	American Library Association
Navigation	Good
Visual Appeal	Fair
Interactive Activity	None

At *Sites for Children: Literature and Language,* the Association for Library Service to Children has brought together a fascinating list of sites under the categories of Favorite Children's Stories, Expanding the Classics, Authors and Illustrators, and Writing by Children. From the first category you can find sites devoted to children's book series such as *The Baby-Sitters' Club* and the *Berenstain Bears.* For *The Lion, The Witch, and the Wardrobe,* which is another of the works listed in the favorite children's stories list, you can find a very detailed and extensive theme unit by Marty Pettigrew, titled *A Journey into Make Believe.* In Expanding the Classics your students can explore, for instance, *The Many Faces of Alice,* a fully illustrated (by students at the Dalton School in New York), full-text version of Lewis Carroll's *Alice's Adventures in Wonderland* accompanied by student essays and a teaching packet.

The Authors and Illustrators section includes lists about many authors such as Katherine Paterson, who wrote *Bridge to Terabithia, The Great Gilly Hopkins, Lyddie,* and *Jacob Have I Loved.* If you would like your students to read stories by other young people, see the Writing by Children sites, which contain many interesting and moving stories. One particularly powerful site is the Diary Project, where your students can read more than 6,000 entries by children and young adults on topics such as family, feelings, friends, school, and racism, and where they may contribute their own diary entries if they wish.

Learning About the Author and Illustrator Pages

http://www.scils.rutgers.edu/special/kay/author.html	
Intended Audience	Teachers and students
Grade Level	4-12
Curricular Fit	Childrens and young adult literature
Types of Resources	Biographical and literary sites
Authorship of Site	Kay Vandergrift
Navigation	Good
Visual Appeal	Good
Interactive Activity	None

Included in the more than 600 sites listed in Kay Vandergrift's *Learning About the Author and Illustrator Pages* are authors and illustrators of children's and young adult books as well as many authors of adult books that are commonly read by older children. As Kay explains, the author/illustrator sites included are not intended to contain comprehensive information about particular authors/illustrators. Rather, some contain biographical, bibliographic, and critical data along with personal responses to selected works, while others provide a small taste of an author's/illustrator's work. This is a rich source of information about the authors of children's and young adult books and illustrators from Lloyd Alexander to Paul Zindel.

Wonderful Wizard of Oz

http://www.eskimo.com/~tiktok/index.html	
Intended Audience	Teachers
Grade Level	4-8
Curricular Fit	Children's fantasy literature
Types of Resources	Excellent set of lessons for theme unit
Authorship of Site	Eric Gjovaag
Navigation	Good
Visual Appeal	Good
Interactive Activity	None

Eric Gjovaag's *Wonderful Wizard of Oz* website contains many fine illustrations and images from various editions of Frank Baum's book and the famous movie that was made from it. At this site you can also discuss Baum's books by joining an e-mail list. Furthermore, you can download an excellent set of theme unit activities that combine activities for science, health, geography, history, mathematics, language arts, art, music, technology, social and life skills, home economics, and psychology. In the list of science activities, for instance, Gjovaag suggests that students get carried away with a study of tornadoes. They can visit a linked tornado page telling them the tornado warning signs and what to do if they are ever caught in a tornado.

Among the language arts activities recommended by Gjovaag is to encourage students to write their own, original Oz adventures. The students can even make themselves the main characters! How did they get there? Who did they meet? What problems did they encounter? How do they get home? The possible story lines are endless.

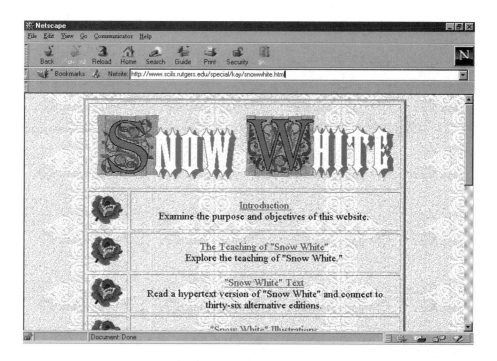

Snow White

http://www.scils.rutgers.edu/special/kay/snowwhite.html	
Intended Audience	Teachers
Grade Level	University Children's Literature Course
Curricular Fit	Fairy tales and folklore
Types of Resources	Critical analyses of Snow White
Authorship of Site	Kay Vandergrift
Navigation	Good
Visual Appeal	Fair
Interactive Activity	None

While the site *Snow White* does not give much direct assistance to those who wish to teach the story to their students, it does provide important critical perspectives on the various versions of the story as well as thought-provoking questions for teachers to consider, such as the following:

■ What are the differences among the textual interpretations of the story?

■ Are the different versions intended for different audiences?

- How do these versions compare with the earliest available written form of the story?
- What are the differences among the visual interpretations of the story?
- Is the specific content of the story altered in any way by the illustrations? If so, how (character, mood, plot, etc.)?
- What is the relationship, if any, between illustrative technique and mood in the story? Between color and mood?
- How are the visual details of setting used in the storytelling?
- Is the number of illustrations and their placement in relation to the text appropriate to the story?
- Do visual and verbal points of view correspond and complement each other?
- Is the format of the book as a physical object part of its affective statement as story?

Storytime

http://www.pbs.org/kcet/storytime/top.htm	
Intended Audience	Teachers and parents
Grade Level	K-2
Curricular Fit	Early literacy
Types of Resources	Short descriptions of story books, literacy advice for parents
Authorship of Site	KCET and PBS
Navigation	Good
Visual Appeal	Good
Interactive Activity	None

The *Storytime* site provides short descriptions of the books that have been read on the PBS television show *Storytime*. Here parents and teachers of primary students can also read helpful suggestions about how to raise their children's literacy levels.

Aesops Fables Online Collection

http://www.pacificnet.net/~johnr/aesop/	
Intended Audience	Teachers and students
Grade Level	2-10
Curricular Fit	Folklore, fairy tales, and fables
Types of Resources	Audioclips, electronic texts, illustrations of the tales
Authorship of Site	John R. Long of Star Systems
Navigation	Good
Visual Appeal	Good
Interactive Activity	Listening to stories and viewing illustrations

Included among the more than 650 fables at *Aesops Fables Online Collection* are Real Audio narrations, classic images, random images, random fables, a search engine, a message forum, and much more on the way. This site also offers 127 fairy tales by Hans Christian Andersen. A particularly endearing feature of the site, which will undoubtedly appeal to younger children, is the narration provided on Real Audio by Heather Long, the 10-year-old daughter of the website's author, John Long.

Reading Zone

http://www.ipl.org/cgi-bin/youth/youth.out.pl?sub=rzn0000	
Intended Audience	Students
Grade Level	4-9
Curricular Fit	Reading
Types of Resources	Picture books, short stories, and poetry
Authorship of Site	Internet Public Library Youth Division
Navigation	Good
Visual Appeal	Good
Interactive Activity	Some opportunity to take part in discussion groups

When your students visit the *Reading Zone* site they can learn how braille works or read picture books such as Toney Lovell's *Jessie the Cow*, the delightful adventure of a cow gone bad. They can also read short stories by children or poems by children and adults. And, for the more advanced readers, there are some deliciously scary ghost stories to be read around the campfire.

Room 108

http://netrover.com/~kingskid/108.html	
Intended Audience	Teachers and students
Grade Level	K-3
Curricular Fit	Reading activities
Types of Resources	Music, stories, games
Authorship of Site	John Rickey
Navigation	Good
Visual Appeal	Good
Interactive Activity	Listening to the songs and viewing the animation

Room 108 is an educational activity center for children. The stories at this site have sound and animation. There are enjoyable games for children, all with an educational focus. This site provides songs and artwork as well.

The Unofficial Beverly Cleary Home Page

http://www.teleport.com/~krp/cleary.html	
Intended Audience	Teachers and students
Grade Level	4-8
Curricular Fit	Children's literature
Types of Resources	Biography, book descriptions, FAQs
Authorship of Site	Karen R. Pederson
Navigation	Good
Visual Appeal	Good
Interactive Activity	None

At *The Unofficial Beverly Cleary home page,* you and your students can learn about the author's life and books. Beverly Cleary cannot answer all the fan mail that she receives each day about her books, so the site has posted the correspondence that some fans have received from her in the past to satisfy the curiosity of young readers.

If you wish to purchase the videos of the PBS television series of Cleary's stories, you can find the address of the films' distributor here. Also, if your students want to learn more about Cleary's wonderful characters, such as Beezus and Ramona Quimby or Henry Huggins, this site has a page (still under construction at the time of this writing) that answers such questions as, "How much is Ramona like her creator?"

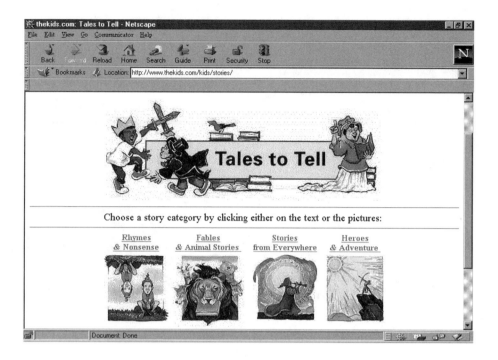

Tales to Tell

http://www.thekids.com/kids/stories/	
Intended Audience	Teachers and Students
Grade Level	K-6
Curricular Fit	Poems, fables, and adventure picture books
Types of Resources	Links to background information about the stories
Authorship of Site	
Navigation	Good
Visual Appeal	Excellent
Interactive Activity	Viewing of animated illustrations and submitting stories

At the *Tales to Tell* site children can read wonderful stories and poems from around the world that are illustrated with animations, and they can submit their own stories to be published here. Some of the stories provided at this site are the French tale, "The Yellow Dwarf," the Native American story, "Osoon Turkey and the Wizard's Heart," and, from *The Thousand and One Nights,* the tale of "The Seven Voyages of Sinbad the Sailor."

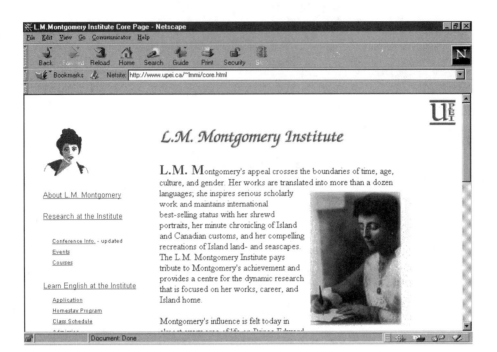

L. M. Montgomery Institute

http://www.upei.ca/~lmmi/core.html	
Intended Audience	Teachers
Grade Level	5-9
Curricular Fit	Canadian literature
Types of Resources	Conferences and teacher resources on books and films
Authorship of Site	L. M. Montgomery Institute
Navigation	Good
Visual Appeal	Good
Interactive Activity	None

The *L.M. Montgomery Institute,* dedicated to Lucy Maud Montgomery, provides you with information about her internationally acclaimed books such as *Anne of Green Gables* and *Emily of New Moon.* You can order videos of the movies based upon her books and teacher's guides to her work. If you wish, you can even arrange to come to an international conference about Montgomery's works and life.

The Page at Pooh Corner

http://chaos.trxinc.com/jmilne/Pooh/	
Intended Audience	Teachers
Grade Level	K-5
Curricular Fit	Children's literature
Types of Resources	Info on books and biographical info about A. A. Milne
Authorship of Site	James Milne
Navigation	Good
Visual Appeal	Good
Interactive Activity	None

The Page at Pooh Corner contains biographical information about A. A. Milne and his son Christopher, who was the inspiration for Christopher Robin in the *Winnie the Pooh* stories. The site's author, James Milne, includes an explanation of the origins of Winnie, an e-mail discussion list about Milne's works, and links to other Winnie the Pooh sites. Lyrics to Pooh's and Tigger's songs and a brief bibliography of books about A. A.'s and Christopher's lives and works are also available here.

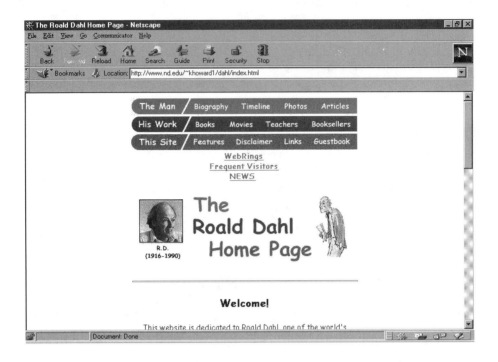

The Roald Dahl Home Page

http://www.nd.edu/~khoward1/dahl/index.html	
Intended Audience	Teachers and students
Grade Level	K-9
Curricular Fit	Children's and young adult literature
Types of Resources	Bio, books, articles, movies, teaching ideas
Authorship of Site	Kristine Howard
Navigation	Good
Visual Appeal	Good
Interactive Activity	Some videoclips and interesting lesson ideas

The Roald Dahl Home Page contains many useful features to help you come to know Roald Dahl and his books. In a moving article by Roald's wife, the actress Patricia Neal, she describes how devastated she and her husband were by the death of their seven-year-old daughter, Olivia, in 1961. Besides the biographical information and articles about Dahl's writing, you can find a number of interesting lesson ideas sent to the site's author by teachers. For instance, one suggested activity to be attempted with children when they are reading *Charlie and the Chocolate Factory* is to let them make up stories about their tour through Mr. Wonka's factory or have them invent their own factories. Links to movies based on Dahl's books include reviews and videoclips of *James and the Giant Peach, Matilda,* and *Willy Wonka and the Chocolate Factory.*

Edward Lear Home Page

http://www2.pair.com/mgraz/Lear/index.html	
Intended Audience	Teachers and students
Grade Level	K-12
Curricular Fit	Nonsense poetry
Types of Resources	Lear's complete limericks and links to related sites
Authorship of Site	Marco Graziosi
Navigation	Good
Visual Appeal	Good
Interactive Activity	None

Marco Graziosi, the author of the *Edward Lear Home Page,* has written a thesis about Lear's nonsense verse, and he wanted to make the poems and Lear's biography available to fellow Lear devotees on the Internet. As Graziosi puts it, "If you share the Jumblies' spirit of adventure or your nose is as luminous as the Dong's, if you think there's nothing strange in living in the nest of an owl or your feelings are wrung with compunction, go on" and enjoy this wonderfully humorous site.

YOUNG ADULT LITERATURE

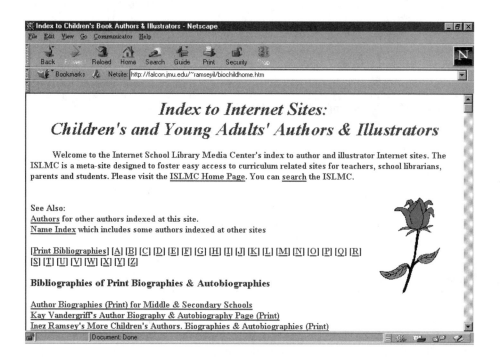

The ISLMC's Children's and Young Adults' Authors & Illustrators

http://falcon.jmu.edu/~ramseyil/biochildhome.htm	
Intended Audience	Teachers and students
Grade Level	K-12
Curricular Fit	Children's and young adult literature
Types of Resources	Bibliographies, biographies, and book reviews
Authorship of Site	Inez Ramsey for the Internet School Library Media Center
Navigation	Good
Visual Appeal	Good
Interactive Activity	None

Inez Ramsey's extensive list of authors of children's and young adult books on the ISLMC Index not only provides excellent biographical and bibliographical materials for each author but also supplies teacher resources for many of the writers as well.

In the case of Lois Lowry, for example, you will find eight different brief biographies, a list of 24 books by Lowry, and 10 teachers' guides about her work. You can also read online reviews of her books and choose from more than 10 unit plans. One of these, on *The Giver*, includes the opportunity for students to listen to an audio file of Lowry discussing her reasons for ending the story as she did before being encouraged to write their own ending to the novel. Inez Ramsey's site is indeed a thorough and valuable resource for K–12 teachers of literature.

Canadian Young Adult Literature

http://canlit.st-john.umanitoba.ca/Canlitx/yauthor.html	
Intended Audience	Teachers and students
Grade Level	8-12
Curricular Fit	Canadian young adult literature
Types of Resources	Author biographies, book reviews
Authorship of Site	Maureen Arnason
Navigation	Good
Visual Appeal	Fair
Interactive Activity	None

The *Canadian Young Adult Literature* site is very helpful in providing basic biographies of Canadian writers of young adult literature and reviews of their books; however, it does not provide links to related sites or teacher resources and lesson plans. Nevertheless, if you use this site as a starting point to identify who the authors are, you can then do a Yahoo search in order to discover that several of these writers have their own websites, such as the following home pages of Paul Kropp and Kevin Major.

Paul Kropp's Web Page

http://www.clo.com/~author/index.html	
Intended Audience	Teachers and students
Grade Level	4-10
Curricular Fit	Young adult high action literature
Types of Resources	Excerpts from books, links to sites for teens
Authorship of Site	Jason and Alex Kropp
Navigation	Good
Visual Appeal	Fair
Interactive Activity	Students can write the author

Paul Kropp has written 38 novels for young adults as well as nonfiction books about schools and reading for parents. He provides excerpts for his most recently published novel and from his current work in progress at his website. He encourages young readers to e-mail him but states that they should ask at least one intelligent question if they wish to receive a reply.

The Novels of Kevin Major

http://www4.newcomm.net/kmajor/	
Intended Audience	Teachers and Students
Grade Level	6-10
Curricular Fit	Young adult literature
Types of Resources	Biographical and bibliographical info and teaching guides
Authorship of Site	Kevin Major
Navigation	Good
Visual Appeal	Good
Interactive Activity	Students can write the author or visit related sites

Kevin Major is a Newfoundland writer of such popular young adult novels as *Diana: My Autobiography.* For four of his novels he provides teaching guides that contain imaginative English language arts and social studies activities as well as interesting links to other sites on the Internet. For example, for his novel, *Blood Red Ochre,* a time-travel novel about the extinction of the Beothuk Aboriginal people of Newfoundland, he suggests that students consider what might have happened had the Beothuks survived. He also provides a link to the Newfoundland and Labrador website, where they can read about the Beothuk people and view some of their artifacts.

Young Adult Literature Library

http://www.uiowa.edu/~english/litcult2097/tlucht/lit-yalib.html	
Intended Audience	Teachers and students
Grade Level	7-12
Curricular Fit	Young adult literature
Types of Resources	Short descriptions of books
Authorship of Site	Thorven Lucht
Navigation	Good
Visual Appeal	Good
Interactive Activity	None

At Thorven Lucht's *Young Adult Literature Library* site you will find short summaries and reviews of more than 30 young adult novels by such famous writers as J. D. Salinger, Robert Cormier, and Peter Dickinson. Lucht says, for instance, of Dickinson's science fiction novel *Eva,* about a teenaged girl whose mind is shifted into the brain of a chimpanzee, that the book "is a very intense read and touches many important issues, most of all the common young adult question of identity, which is very central for Eva, being torn between two worlds."

Random House's Alphabetical Title Index of Young Adult Literature Guides

http://www.randomhouse.com/teachersbdd/trc_alphabetical.html	
Intended Audience	Teachers
Grade Level	7-12
Curricular Fit	Young adult literature
Types of Resources	Teaching guides for 100 Random House novels
Authorship of Site	Random House
Navigation	Good
Visual Appeal	Fair
Interactive Activity	None

Random House's Index provides a list of teaching resources for approximately 100 young adult novels by such well-known authors as Madeleine L'Engle, S. E. Hinton, and Gary Paulsen. It enables, for instance, teachers of the Hinton novels, *Tex, Rumble Fish,* and *Taming the Star Runner,* to encourage their students to consider the themes of acceptance, family relationships, self-esteem, and self-discovery in these three books, as well as to examine interdisciplinary links with history and science.

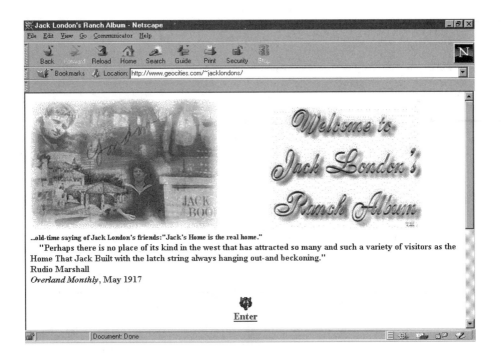

Welcome to Jack London's Ranch Album

http://www.geocities.com/~jacklondons/	
Intended Audience	Teachers
Grade Level	6-12
Curricular Fit	Young adult fiction
Types of Resources	Pictures, biography, electronic versions of London's books
Authorship of Site	David Hartzell
Navigation	Good
Visual Appeal	Good
Interactive Activity	None

This site is an excellent resource for students who want to read Jack London's books and to learn about his adventurous life. Among the texts students can read here in electronic form are *The Call of the Wild, The Sea-Wolf,* and *Selected Klondike Stories.* They can also learn about the model farm that London was working on before he died at the age of 40.

Gary Paulsen

http://www.randomhouse.com/features/garypaulsen/	
Intended Audience	Teachers and students
Grade Level	6-10
Curricular Fit	Young adult literature
Types of Resources	Biography of Paulsen and descriptions of his books
Authorship of Site	Random House
Navigation	Good
Visual Appeal	Good
Interactive Activity	None

At the Gary Paulsen site students can read about Gary's exciting boat trip in the South Pacific, and they can send him questions about his novel *Hatchet* and the sequel he recently completed, *Brian's Return*. They can also visit the *Library* section of the site to learn about some of Paulsen's other novels.

Lois Duncan

http://www.iag.net/~barq/lois.html	
Intended Audience	Teachers and students
Grade Level	7-10
Curricular Fit	Young adult literature
Types of Resources	Author biography and book summaries
Authorship of Site	Lois Duncan
Navigation	Good
Visual Appeal	Good
Interactive Activity	None

On the first page of Lois Duncan's site she writes a letter to her young fans in which she talks about the violence in her books. A sixth-grade student wrote to tell her that his father was trying to have one of her books, *Killing Mr. Griffin*, banned in Alabama schools. Lois points out that she, too, feels that the book is inappropriate for sixth graders to read but that it is fine for grade 7 and 8 students. She wrote a non-fiction book titled *Who Killed My Daughter?* about the murder of her teenaged daughter, and so she is quite aware of the horrors of violence in society. Nevertheless, she feels that her books help teens to think about the consequences of the violence that is a part of their world. This site contains a brief biography of Lois Duncan and short descriptions of her books.

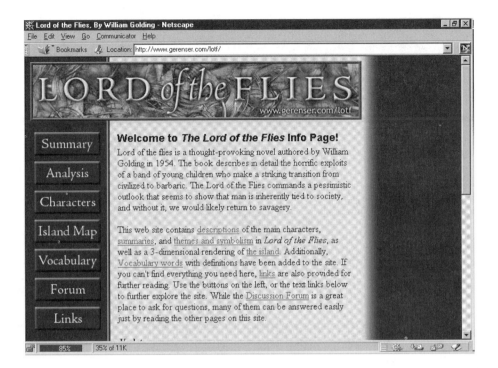

Lord of the Flies

http://www.gerenser.com/lotf/	
Intended Audience	Teachers and students
Grade Level	10-12
Curricular Fit	Young adult literature
Types of Resources	Author bio, overview, character sketches, symbolism chart
Authorship of Site	Scott Gerenser
Navigation	Good
Visual Appeal	Good
Interactive Activity	Discussion Forum

Students who visit the *Lord of the Flies* site can study vocabulary lists for each chapter, post their ideas and questions about the book on a discussion forum, read summaries of the book's chapters, see photographs and read descriptions of the main characters, and follow links to sites about the life of the book's author, William Golding.

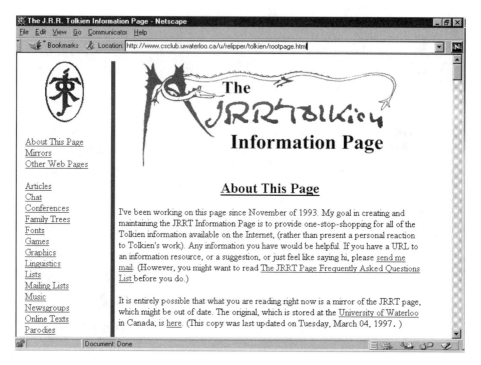

The J.R.R. Tolkien Information Page

http://www.csclub.uwaterloo.ca/u/relipper/tolkien/rootpage.html	
Intended Audience	Teachers and students
Grade Level	6-12
Curricular Fit	Young adult literature
Types of Resources	Links to dozens of Tolkien Sites
Authorship of Site	Eric Lippert
Navigation	Good
Visual Appeal	Good
Interactive Activity	Games and a recording of Tolkien's last interview

This *J.R.R. Tolkien Information Page* provides links to dozens of other sites about Tolkien's *Lord of the Rings* and *The Hobbit*. There are many links to articles, elvish fonts, graphics, games, and music. This page also provides extensive lists of Tolkien newsgroups, periodicals, and societies, as well as links to linguistics sites about the languages in Tolkien's novels. Related sites include pages devoted to the works of C.S. Lewis. And under the category of miscellaneous sites is a link to a recording and transcript of the last interview ever given by J.R.R. Tolkien.

SF Lovers

http://sflovers.rutgers.edu/.index2.html	
Intended Audience	Science fiction readers of all ages
Grade Level	8-12
Curricular Fit	Young adult literature
Types of Resources	Back issues SF Lovers electronic journal, many good links
Authorship of Site	Saul Jaffe
Navigation	Good
Visual Appeal	Good
Interactive Activity	None

The *SF Lovers* site contains a wonderful list of links to sites that are of interest to those who love to read and view science fiction. These links include winners of the Hugo awards, reference materials about authors and books, materials from book publishers, information about science fiction films and television shows, science fiction, fantasy and horror artwork, and fan activities, including conventions.

Science Fiction Resource Guide

http;//sflovers.rutgers.edu/archive/Web/SFRG/sf-resource.guide.html	
Intended Audience	Science fiction readers of all ages
Grade Level	8-12
Curricular Fit	Young adult fiction
Types of Resources	A wealth of links to science fiction related sites
Authorship of Site	Chaz Boston Baden
Navigation	Good
Visual Appeal	Good
Interactive Activity	Role playing, group writing, listening to audio files

Like the *SF Lovers* page, the *Science Fiction Resource Guide* contains an extensive list of author's pages and related sites. But this site also provides visitors with access to science fiction role-playing games, electronic magazines, and comics. As well, it has various audio files of music and radio shows. In a section titled *Notes War*, visitors to the site are encouraged to take part with other visitors in the ongoing writing of a piece of science fiction. In another section students can read complete works and serialized works of science fiction. Finally, your students can find here advice to aspiring science fiction writers.

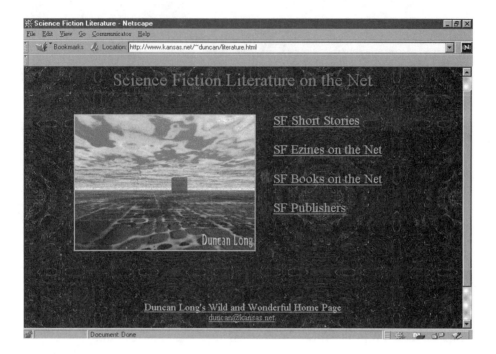

Science Fiction Literature on the Net

http://www.kansas.net/~duncan/literature.html	
Intended Audience	Mature science fiction readers
Grade Level	10-12
Curricular Fit	Young adult literature
Types of Resources	Science fiction short stories, ezines, books, and publishers
Authorship of Site	Duncan Long
Navigation	Good
Visual Appeal	Good
Interactive Activity	None

Duncan Long's science fiction site, *Science Fiction Literature on the Net,* is not as extensive or interactive as the previous two sites, but its pages are more attractive for adolescent readers. Long adds several of his own stories to those of Edgar Allan Poe, H. G. Wells, Ambrose Bierce, and others. He also provides readers with many links to science fiction novels, e-zines, and publishers. This site is not recommended for students under the age of 16 because of the graphic descriptions of violence in some of the stories.

Arthur C. Clarke Unauthorized Home Page

http://www.lsi.usp.br/~rbianchi/clarke/	
Intended Audience	Adolescent science fiction readers
Grade Level	8-12
Curricular Fit	Young adult literature
Types of Resources	Biography, bibliography, filmography, interviews
Authorship of Site	Reinaldo Bianchi
Navigation	Good
Visual Appeal	Good
Interactive Activity	None

This site contains an large collection of sites about the author and his works as well as links to information about the films that have been based upon his novels, such as *2001: A Space Odyssey.* Students with a real interest in Clarke's work may wish to join the Arthur C. Clarke Fan Club.

Robert Heinlein: Dean of Science Fiction Writers

http://www.wegrokit.com	
Intended Audience	Science fiction readers
Grade Level	7-12
Curricular Fit	Young adult literature
Types of Resources	Biography, bibliography, audio file, bulletin board, news
Authorship of Site	Lizbeth Ager and Carlos Angelo
Navigation	Good
Visual Appeal	Good
Interactive Activity	Listening to radio show

This site provides an examination of Heinlein's life and legacy and an extensive collection of book reviews, excerpts, and book covers. Essays about Heinlein, his works and his influence, a bulletin board, and the weekly *Heinlein News* all combine to furnish readers with a rich assortment of background materials with which to assess his fiction. Among the many related sites linked to this one are an audio file of a radio play version of Heinlein's classic short story, "The Roads Must Roll," and a New Age Church of All Worlds named after a church in Heinlein's novel *Stranger in a Strange Land.*

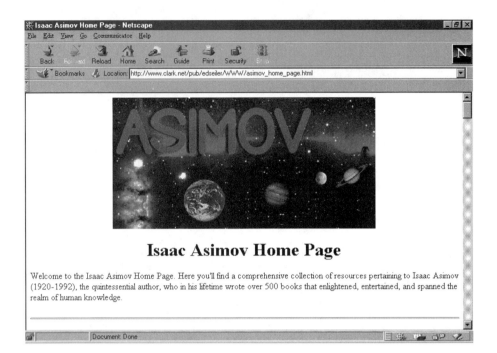

Isaac Asimov Home Page

http://www.clark.net/pub/edseiler/WWW/asimov_home_page.html	
Intended Audience	Science fiction readers
Grade Level	8-12
Curricular Fit	Young adult literature
Types of Resources	FAQs, descriptions of his books, reviews, audio files
Authorship of Site	Edward Seiler
Navigation	Good
Visual Appeal	Good
Interactive Activity	None

Because Isaac Asimov wrote over 500 books during his lifetime, it is understandable that this site dedicated to his works would be so rich with information. From here your students can download a transcript and audio file of a speech delivered by Asimov, they can read reviews and essays about his more famous books such as the *Foundation* series, and they can read answers to a huge list of FAQs about his life and work. Among the related sites available through the home page is the electronic magazine titled *Science Fiction Weekly*.

The Unofficial Ursula K. Le Guin Page

http://www.wenet.net/~lquilter/femsf/authors/leguin/	
Intended Audience	Teachers and students
Grade Level	4-12
Curricular Fit	Children's and Young Adult Science Fiction
Types of Resources	Biography, bibliography, interviews, performances, reviews
Authorship of Site	Laura Quilter
Navigation	Good
Visual Appeal	Fair
Interactive Activity	None

As one of the Ursula Le Guin's interviewers points out in this site, she is the prolific high priestess of science fiction. She has written more than 16 novels, 4 collections of poetry, 10 children's books, several screenplays, and more. This site provides brief descriptions of Le Guin's children's and young adult science fiction books as well as a list of the television performances of her books, such as *The Lathe of Heaven*. Although there are some good links to sources of information about Le Guin and her books, most of the resources on this site are lists of books and articles that must be obtained from libraries. For Le Guin fans these are nevertheless valuable lists.

PERNtinent Information

http://home.earthlink.net/~lessa/	
Intended Audience	Students
Grade Level	5-9
Curricular Fit	Young adult fantasy fiction
Types of Resources	Newsgroups, fantasy art, book descriptions
Authorship of Site	Lisa Spencer
Navigation	Good
Visual Appeal	Good
Interactive Activity	None

Students can find here descriptions of Anne McCaffrey's many dragon books, and they can join the alt.pern.fan newsgroup to send and receive e-mail about McCaffrey's series of fantasy books such as *The Dragonriders of Pern*. By visiting the many linked Pern sites, students can see an extensive list of all of the characters in the Pern books, poetry inspired by McCaffrey's world of Pern, and thousands of images of dragons.

MYTHOLOGY

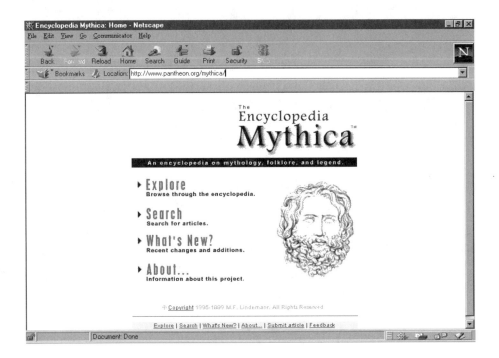

The Encyclopedia Mythica

http://www.pantheon.org/mythica/	
Intended Audience	Teachers and students
Grade Level	4-12
Curricular Fit	Mythology
Types of Resources	Articles, images, maps, genealogical tables, links
Authorship of Site	M.F. Lindemans
Navigation	Good
Visual Appeal	Good
Interactive Activity	None

The *Encylopedia Mythica* contains over 4,700 articles on mythological characters from around the world. Greek, Chinese, Aztec, Hindu, and Celtic mythologies are just a few of the many represented here. Students can also view over 200 beautiful illustrations, maps, and genealogical tables.

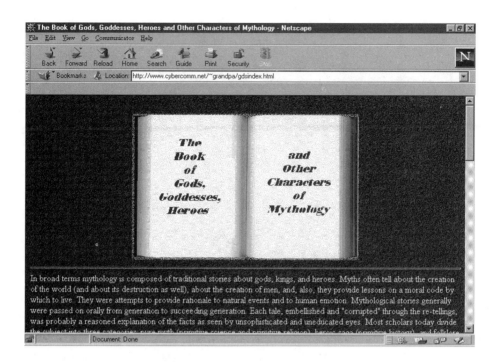

The Book of Gods, Goddesses, Heroes, and Other Characters of Mythology

http://www.cybercomm.net/~grandpa/gdsindex.html	
Intended Audience	Teachers and Students
Grade Level	4-12
Curricular Fit	Mythology
Types of Resources	Character lists, stories, images, 150 world mythologies links
Authorship of Site	P.J. Criss
Navigation	Good
Visual Appeal	Good
Interactive Activity	None

This site is even more encyclopedic than the previous one, as visitors are invited to study mythological characters from around the world, view their images, and read their stories. But the best feature of this site is its list of 150 other mythology sites, organized by cultural regions (Asian, African, etc.). For ease of navigation the web site author has gathered the materials for this *Book of Gods* into chapters on Characters, Myths, Folklore, Creatures, Epics, The Gods, Gallery, and Links.

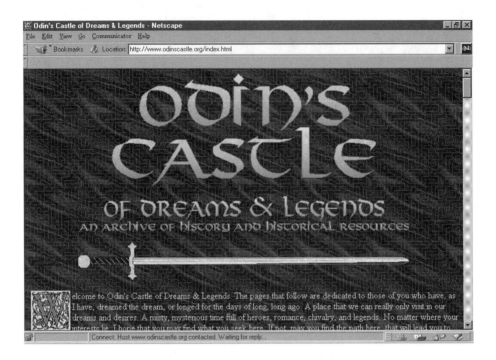

Odin's Castle of Dreams and Legends: An Archive of History and Historical Resources

http://www.odinscastle.org/index.html	
Intended Audience	Teachers and Students
Grade Level	6-12
Curricular Fit	Interdisciplinary theme units: mythology, legends, history
Types of Resources	Links to mythological and historical sites
Authorship of Site	Paul Gwynn
Navigation	Good
Visual Appeal	Good
Interactive Activity	None

Odin's Castle is the remarkably ambitious creation of education doctoral student and Vietnam veteran Paul Gwynn. We include it here because of the wonderful array of mythological links that Gwynn has stored in the castle's armory. But this site is primarily dedicated to making history attractive to students of all ages, so we recommend it as well as an excellent source of historical information for interdisciplinary theme units.

In the mythology section of Odin's Castle your students can find links, for example, to Folklore and Mythology Electronic Texts, Beowulf, Faerie Lore and Literature, Werewolf Legends from Germany, Irish Folklore, Voodoo, and Conan the Barbarian. His goal is clearly to both delight and instruct as he provides access through his extensive list of links to everything "from the top of Olympus to the depths of Dr. Frankenstein's laboratory."

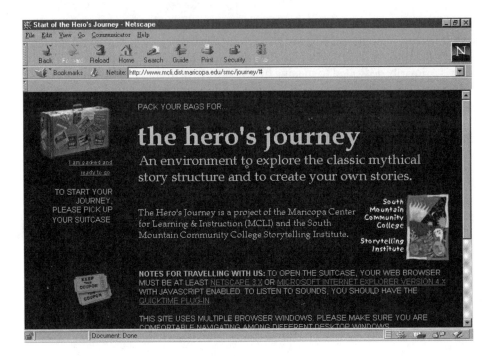

The Hero's Journey

http://www.mcli.dist.maricopa.edu/smc/journey/#	
Intended Audience	Teachers and students
Grade Level	8-12
Curricular Fit	Mythology and creative writing
Types of Resources	A list of questions and sample stories to guide myth writing
Authorship of Site	Alan Levine
Navigation	Good
Visual Appeal	Good
Interactive Activity	Students can post stories and interpretations at the site

The Hero's Journey is an interactive site in which students can use a story tool consisting of a set of questions based upon the theories in Joseph Campbell's book, *The Hero with a Thousand Faces,* either to construct their own heroic tales or to analyze the structure of classical myths and legends.

POETRY

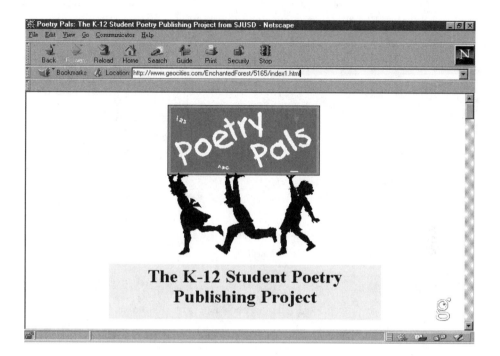

Poetry Pals: The K–12 Student Poetry Publishing Project

http://www.geocities.com/EnchantedForest/5165/index1.html	
Intended Audience	Teachers and students
Grade Level	K-12
Curricular Fit	Creative Writing
Types of Resources	Poems from around the world and info about countries
Authorship of Site	C. Markham
Navigation	Good
Visual Appeal	Good
Interactive Activity	Students can read each other's poems and exchange e-mail

At The *Poetry Pals* site your students can read poetry by K–12 students from around the world. A few of the countries represented are Canada, the United States,

Australia, England, El Slavador, Japan, and Russia. Students are shown how to write a variety of styles of poetry, including haiku and limericks. Many different lesson plans and related sites are available for teachers to explore. For example, one lesson plan recommends that students locate an autobiographical poem written by a student from a different country. Then they are to compare how the author is alike and different from themselves by listing unique and shared characteristics.

A Haiku Homepage

http://home.clara.net/pka/haiku/haiku.htm	
Intended Audience	Teachers and students
Grade Level	8-12
Curricular Fit	Creative writing
Types of Resources	Links to famous haiku poets, amateur poets' contributions
Authorship of Site	Phil Adams
Navigation	Good
Visual Appeal	Fair
Interactive Activity	Visiting poets can post their haiku at this page

Phil Adams has created a page from which you and your students can explore haiku and contribute their own poems to the page. The poems at this site would be less likely to appeal to younger children than to adolescents because of their sophistication and understatement. Your students will find here a nice combination of ancient and contemporary, professional and amateur poems.

The Academy of American Poets—Poetry Gallery

http://www.poets.org/lit/litmain.htm	
Intended Audience	Teachers and students
Grade Level	9-12
Curricular Fit	American poets
Types of Resources	List of American poets and their works, audio files of poems
Authorship of Site	The Academy of American Poets
Navigation	Good
Visual Appeal	Fair
Interactive Activity	Listening to famous poets read their works

The *Academy of American Poets* page contains a large collection of audio files of famous authors such as Robert Frost, e. e. cummings, and T.S. Eliot reading their poems. Students can follow along with their eyes, scanning the text on the screen while they listen to the poets' interpretive readings. It is truly fascinating to be able to hear the voices of these writers.

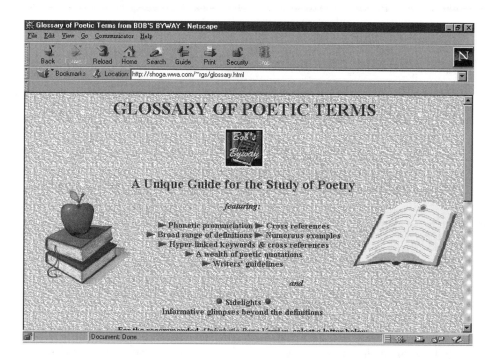

Glossary of Poetic Terms

http://shoga.wwa.com/~rgs/glossary.html	
Intended Audience	Teachers and students
Grade Level	9-12
Curricular Fit	Poetry reading
Types of Resources	Hypertextually link set of poetic terms and poems
Authorship of Site	Robert G. Shubinski
Navigation	Good
Visual Appeal	Good
Interactive Activity	None

In the *Glossary of Poetic Terms* your students can study a particular poetic device by reading a definition of the term that contains links to other related terms and also provides an example from a poem. Thus they can learn that a *caesura* is a "rhythmic break or pause in the flow of *sound* which is commonly introduced in about the middle of a line of verse," and they are encouraged to follow a hyperlink to the word *sound*. A second hypertextual link takes them to the Emily Dickinson poem, "I'm Nobody! Who are You?" which contains a caesura in its first line. This is a very effective way to enable students to learn important poetic terms.

Twentieth-Century Poetry in English

http://www.lit.kobe-u.ac.jp/~hishika/20c_poet.htm	
Intended Audience	Teachers and students
Grade Level	10-12
Curricular Fit	Modern poetry
Types of Resources	E-texts of poems, literary criticism, 170 authors biographies
Authorship of Site	Eiichi Hishikawa
Navigation	Good
Visual Appeal	Good
Interactive Activity	None

Professor Eiichi Hishikawa of Kobe University in Japan has provided in this site special pages devoted to 11 famous poets such as W. H. Auden and William Butler Yeats. Links are included as well to 159 other twentieth-century poets. He has also inserted into his pages e-text versions of many poems by these authors and links to other interesting sites about their lives and works. Literary criticism by and about these authors is included as well as extensive bibliographies.

SHORT STORIES

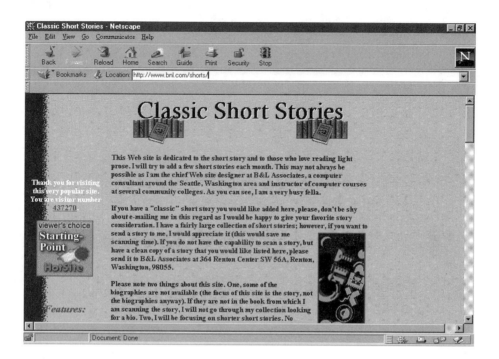

Classic Short Stories

http://www.bnl.com/shorts/	
Intended Audience	Teachers and students
Grade Level	8-12
Curricular Fit	Short stories
Types of Resources	E-texts of classic short stories
Authorship of Site	Gary Lindquist
Navigation	Good
Visual Appeal	Good
Interactive Activity	None

This site contains the e-text versions of more than 65 short stories by masters of the genre such as Edgar Allan Poe and Guy de Maupassant. There are no critical materials included, but a bibliography is provided that gives the original sources of many of the stories. Most of these tales are still taught in high schools and continue to entertain adolescents.

The Moonlit Road

http://www.themoonlitroad.com/ibo/intro_ibo001.html	
Intended Audience	Teachers and students
Grade Level	6-12
Curricular Fit	Short stories—supernatural and suspense
Types of Resources	Audio files and e-text of stories
Authorship of Site	The Moonlit Road Bookshop
Navigation	Good
Visual Appeal	Good
Interactive Activity	Listening to and reading ghost stories from America's South

Each month *The Moonlit Road* features ghost stories and strange folktales from the American South, which are told by the region's best storytellers. By simply selecting stories, your students can hear the storytellers recount their ghostly tales. The stories featured on this site change each month, so you may need to check to see if the particular tales that are available when you want to take your students to this site are appropriate.

NOVELS

Project Gutenberg Electronic Texts

http://promo.net/pg/history.html	
Intended Audience	University students
Grade Level	4-12
Curricular Fit	British and American literature prior to 1950
Types of Resources	E-texts of English literature classics
Authorship of Site	Michael Hart
Navigation	Good
Visual Appeal	Fair
Interactive Activity	None

Whether you want to read the electronic text of William Blake's *Songs of Innocence and Experience* or Edith Nesbit's *Five Children and It,* you can find classics of all kinds at the *Project Gutenberg* page. Begun in 1971 by Michael Hart, this project has over the years attempted to store electronic versions of many of the world's classics

in English. Your students can discover here the full-text versions of hundreds of famous works, and they can navigate their way through those books by using one of
the edit functions in their Netscape browser. For instance, if they want to determine
how many references there are to *blood* in Shakespeare's *Macbeth*, then they can use
Netscape's "find in page" function to conduct a search of Project Gutenberg's e-text
version of the play. From Robert Louis Stevenson's *A Child's Garden of Verses* to
Jonathan Swift's *Gulliver's Travels*, this is the ultimate site for e-texts of the classics of
English literature.

EducETH Reading List For Class Use

http://educeth.ethz.ch/english/readinglist/	
Intended Audience	Teachers and students
Grade Level	10-12
Curricular Fit	American and British literature
Types of Resources	Book summaries, lesson plans, discussion lists
Authorship of Site	Hans G. Fischer
Navigation	Good
Visual Appeal	Fair
Interactive Activity	Students can ask questions about commonly studied texts

This site contains a list of more than 70 of the most commonly studied novels in senior high school English literature classes. Everything from Chinua Achebe's *Things
Fall Apart* to John Wyndham's *The Chrysalids* is included in this helpful site. If we
consider one work, Alice Walker's *The Color Purple*, for example, your students can
read a synopsis of the novel, biographical sketches of the author, critical commen-
tary about the book, poems by Walker about racism, comments and questions by
other students about the book, and a description of the movie directed by Stephen
Spielberg that was based upon the book. This site is particularly useful for new
teachers who are confronted with teaching the regular canon of senior high school
literary texts for the first time and need to access some basic materials about these
texts to aid them in their lesson planning. It is also of course a valuable site for students to visit who want to ask questions of other students about these texts.

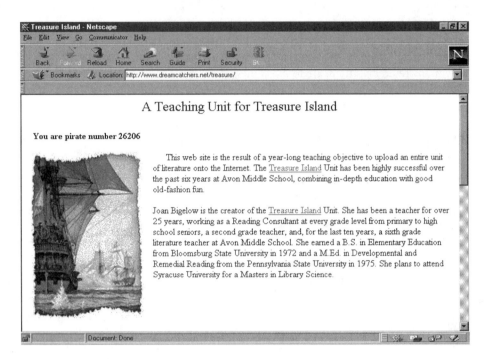

A Teaching Unit for Treasure Island

http://www.dreamcatchers.net/treasure/	
Intended Audience	Teachers and students
Grade Level	6-9
Curricular Fit	Novel study and pirate theme unit
Types of Resources	Questions about pirates, map, puppet show ideas
Authorship of Site	Joan Bigelow
Navigation	Good
Visual Appeal	Good
Interactive Activity	Constructing a Jolly Roger, researching a pirate, etc.

In this fun-filled site students carry out in-depth research on a pirate or a topic related to pirates, learn 30 or more basic parts of a schooner, hear treachery from within an apple barrel, design a personal Jolly Roger, bury treasure sought by ten surly pirates, eat limes and lemons to prevent scurvy, and discover a skeleton pointing the way to a fortune in gold, silver, and jewels. In other words, they have a good deal of fun absorbing knowledge connected with the classic novel, *Treasure Island*.

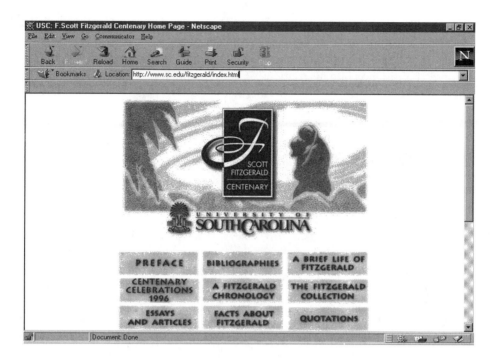

F. Scott Fitzgerald Centenary

http://www.sc.edu/fitzgerald/index.html	
Intended Audience	Students and teachers
Grade Level	11-12
Curricular Fit	American literature
Types of Resources	Biography, bibliography of works by and about Fitzgerald
Authorship of Site	Board of Trustees of the University of South Carolina
Navigation	Good
Visual Appeal	Good
Interactive Activity	Audio and videoclips of Fitzgerald

This site and the *Treasure Island* page are examples of rich resources about one or a few novels by particular authors. If you perform a web search using Yahoo, AltaVista, and other search engines, you can sometimes find sites of this sort by simply typing in the title of the work or the name of the author. In the case of the *F. Scott Fitzgerald Centenary* site, your students will discover a biography of Fitzgerald, a bibliography of works by and about him, several lengthy essays that discuss his novels, audio files of Fitzgerald reading poetry by Keats, Masefield, and Shakespeare, and a video-clip of the author in the 1920s. The University of North Carolina has also provided famous quotes by Fitzgerald and facts about the author that provide readers with glimpses, for instance, into his relationship with Hemingway.

DRAMA

Readers Theatre Online Canada

http://loiswalker.com/catalog/index.html	
Intended Audience	Teachers and Students
Grade Level	K-12
Curricular Fit	Drama in the English Language Arts classroom
Types of Resources	Scripts for all grades as well as ESL and French scripts
Authorship of Site	Lois Walker
Navigation	Good
Visual Appeal	Good
Interactive Activity	8 free scripts for immediate use, many more for purchase

Lois Walker's site contains eight free K–12 *Readers Theatre* scripts for immediate use and many more for purchase. These often humorous texts provide a pleasurable vehicle for improving your students oral reading and interpretation skills. Walker has also made available scripts for French and ESL classes.

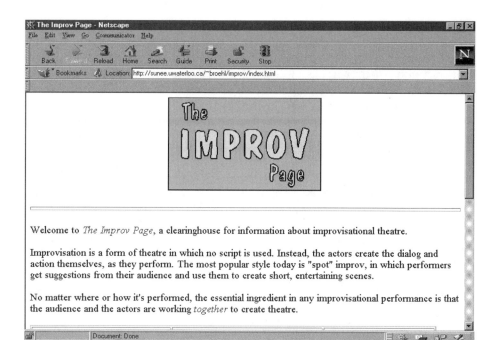

The Improv Page

http://sunee.uwaterloo.ca/~broehl/improv/index.html	
Intended Audience	Teachers and students
Grade Level	K-12
Curricular Fit	Drama in the English and Theatre Arts classroom
Types of Resources	Many teaching ideas for improvisation activities
Authorship of Site	Bernie Roehl
Navigation	Good
Visual Appeal	Fair
Interactive Activity	None at the computer but much in the English classroom

It is not always essential for English language arts sites to involve on-screen interactivity. In *The Improv Page*, for example, you will find no audio or video clips, nor will you even find any pictures or animations. But the words at this site provide excellent opportunities for students to interact with texts, with fellow actors, and with their audience in wonderfully imaginative ways. Besides providing links to sites about improv artists, information about the history of improvisation, and a list of improv terms, this site contains links to lists of well over 300 different improv games and activities for your students to enjoy. For instance, in a game titled Dubbing, off-stage improvisors provide the voices for the onstage characters and action. This activity may also be performed as a foreign film. Or, in another variation, the voice players do not watch the scene and therefore may contradict it. The body players must physically justify what they are saying.

The Dramatic Exchange Catalogue of Plays

http://www.dramex.org/htmlplays.html	
Intended Audience	Teachers and students
Grade Level	K-12
Curricular Fit	Drama in the English and Theatre Arts classroom
Types of Resources	E-texts of more than 300 plays
Authorship of Site	Mike Dederian and Rob Knop
Navigation	Good
Visual Appeal	Fair
Interactive Activity	Reading Plays

Many English and drama teachers have been in the difficult position of attempting to find an appropriate play to use with their English or theater arts classes or in a school Drama Club production. Unfortunately, the one-paragraph descriptions found in traditional sources of plays, such as the *Samuel French Catalogue,* do not provide enough information about the plays to indicate clearly whether or not they will prove suitable. At the *Dramatic Exchange* site, instead of trying to guess about the quality of a play through a single paragraph, you can find both a short description and the entire text of more than 300 contemporary plays. The plays are organized according to the following categories: comedies, tragedies, mysteries, dramas, one-acts, full-length plays, musicals, children's theater, plays for screen, audience participation, and experimental plays. At the *Dramatic Exchange* you can skim through entire plays until you find the ones you want.

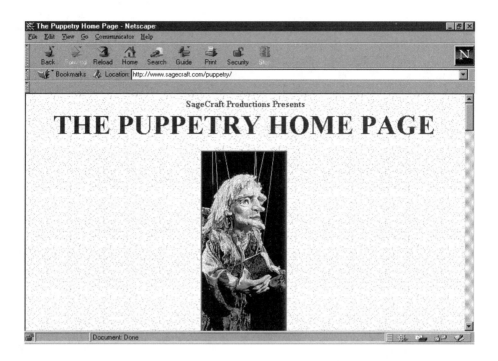

The Puppetry Home Page

http://www.sagecraft.com/puppetry/	
Intended Audience	Teachers and students
Grade Level	K-12
Curricular Fit	Puppets may be used in any Language Arts course
Types of Resources	Definitions, traditions, museums, performances
Authorship of Site	Sagecraft Productions
Navigation	Good
Visual Appeal	Good
Interactive Activity	Students can build their own puppets and perform plays

At this beautifully illustrated site you and your students can learn about puppetry organizations, festivals, and theatres. You can study definitions, worldwide traditions, and schools of puppetry. You can also visit exhibits and museums about puppets. You can learn how to build puppets, and you can find out about various performance companies, sites, and resources. With the help of this site, you and your students can build your own puppets and perform plays in a number of different styles and traditions such as the Balinese Shadow puppets, Japanese Bunraku puppets, and English Punch and Judy puppets. This site is truly a feast for the imagination.

Medieval Drama Links

http://www.leeds.ac.uk/theatre/emd/links.htm	
Intended Audience	Teachers and students
Grade Level	6-12
Curricular Fit	Integrated Medieval theme unit or history of the theatre
Types of Resources	Manuscripts, e-texts of plays, music,
Authorship of Site	Sydney Higgins
Navigation	Good
Visual Appeal	Good
Interactive Activity	Listening to music, viewing paintings and manuscripts

If you are teaching the history of the theater to your theater arts students or if you are planning to raise money for your school by hosting a Medieval Fair, this *Medieval Drama Links* site is the place to visit. Here your students can view medieval costumes and armor, listen to music from medieval instruments such as the crumhorn, learn how to do medieval dances, and examine medieval paintings and sculptures. They can read beautifully illuminated medieval manuscripts and study plays such as *Everyman*. Finally, your students can learn about how to perform the plays, design sets, construct props and apply makeup, and they can join discussion groups and read scholarly journals about medieval drama.

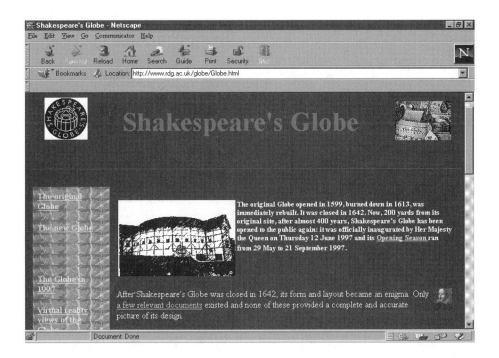

Shakespeare's Globe

http://www.rdg.ac.uk/globe/Globe.html	
Intended Audience	Teachers and Students
Grade Level	9-12
Curricular Fit	Shakespeare in English and Theatre Arts courses
Types of Resources	Virtual tour of the Globe, photos, cultural background info
Authorship of Site	Chantal Miller-Schutz
Navigation	Good
Visual Appeal	Good
Interactive Activity	Students can wander through the new Globe Theatre

What better way to introduce your grade 9 students to Shakespeare than to give them a virtual tour of the newly constructed Globe Theatre in England. At this site, which contains images and background information about Sam Wanamaker's recreation of Shakespeare's original Globe Theatre, your students can also learn about Shakespeare's London.

BRITISH AUTHORS

British and Irish Authors on the Web

http://lang.nagoya-u.ac.jp/~matsuoka/UK-authors.html

The *British and Irish Authors on the Web* site lists authors chronologically from the year 600 AD to the present. The site itself contains only a list of hyperlinks to other sites, but what a list! From its first site on *Beowulf*, where your students can read *Beowulf* in the original Old English or do a word search in a modern English translation, to one of the most recent entries (as of this writing), where they can learn about some of Kazuo Ishiguro's works such as his Booker Prize–winning novel, *The Remains of the Day*, your students have literally hundreds of wonderful British and Irish authors' sites to choose from.

The Shakespeare Resource Center

http://home.earthlink.net/~feiffor/bard/body.html

This site deals not only with Shakespeare's literature, but also with Shakespeare as a man and the environment in which he lived and wrote. It has a built-in search tool to help your students find information about Shakespeare's life and works more easily. By referring to linked sites on other Elizabethan authors such as Christopher Marlowe and Francis Bacon, your students can consider the validity of arguments in the debate about whether or not all of the plays attributed to Shakespeare were actually written by him. As well, they can learn about the nuances of Elizabethan English.

Poor Yorick CD and Video Emporium

http://www.cyg.net/~yorick/home.html

This site is useful for students, teachers, and school librarians who wish to purchase CDs and videos concerning Shakespeare's plays. The site's *Shakespeare Multimedia Catalog* povides public access to a myriad of interpretations and entertainments. The goal of the site's authors is to assist the ever growing academic fields pertaining to Shakespeare in performance and popular culture by providing scholars with the tools they require.

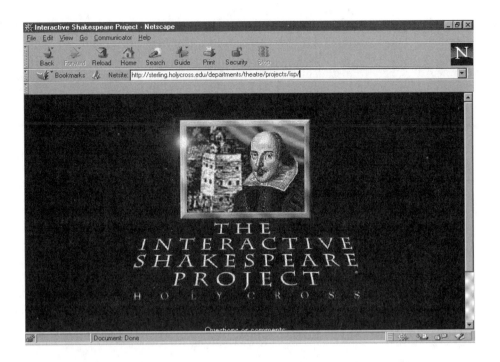

The Interactive Shakespeare Project

http://sterling.holycross.edu/departments/theatre/projects/isp/

Although at the time of writing, this site is focused only upon Shakespeare's play *Measure for Measure,* the authors have plans to include other plays by Shakespeare in the near future. Even if you are not teaching *Measure for Measure,* you should see how this site combines text, video, performance activities, and pedagogical resources with interactive elements. According to the authors, secondary school students who visit the site can control their own learning experience while being exposed to a variety of historical, performance, and textual issues that surround an individual Shakespearean play. Its online *Teacher's Guide* covers such topics as teaching meter, soliloquy preparation, interpretation, writing and using reviews, and performance exercises.

The Bronte Sisters Web

http://lang.nagoya-u.ac.jp/~matsuoka/Bronte.html

Among the e-texts available at the *Bronte Sisters Web Site* are the novels *Jane Eyre* by Charlotte and *Wuthering Heights* by Emily. If you are planning to have your students read either of these novels, it is likely that you have provided them with a paperback version. Nevertheless, when they wish to do research into the appearance of certain important words in these novels, by performing a simple electronic word search they can easily discover for themselves, for instance, that there are more than 100 references to the word "fire" in *Jane Eyre*. As well as studying the novels of the Bronte sisters, here your students can read poems by Charlotte, Emily, and Anne or they can study a fascinating book-length biography of Charlotte published in 1857, just two years after her death, by her friend, Mrs. Elizabeth Gaskell. There are also many other excellent resources on this page, such as a painting of the Brontes and a photograph of the parsonage where they grew up.

The Dickens Page

http://lang.nagoya-u.ac.jp/~matsuoka/Dickens.html

From the Dickens home page your students can access e-texts of several of Charles Dickens' books such as *Great Expectations* and *Oliver Twist*. They can also hear readings by an actor of short passages from *A Christmas Carol,* and they can read an e-text book-length biography of Dickens written in 1874 by his friend, John Forster. Pictures of his family, a concordance, bibliogaphy, and message board are here as well. If you would like to order a film version of one of his books, the Dickens Filmography lists more than 80 films.

Thomas Hardy Resources Library

http://pages.ripco.com:8080/~mws/hardy.html

The *Thomas Hardy Resources Library* contains e-texts of Hardy's novels such as *Tess of the d'Urbervilles* and *The Mayor of Casterbridge* as well as articles about his works and life. If your students wish to learn more about the many wonderful film adaptations of his novels, this site provides links to information on the film versions, for example, of *Jude the Obscure* and *Far from the Madding Crowd*. By going to the pages of information on Wessex, students can compare Hardy's fictional locations with their modern counterparts.

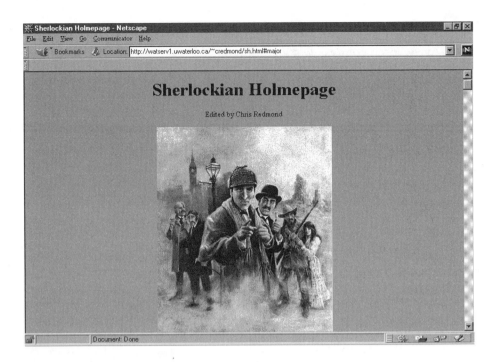

Sherlockian Holmepage

http://watserv1.uwaterloo.ca/~credmond/sh.html

Reputed to be one of the best of many *Sherlock Holmes* pages on the Internet, Chris Redmond's *Sherlockian Holmepage* contains links to hundreds of other Holmes pages that your students can visit. For example, through these links they can take a virtual tour of the Sherlock Holmes Museum, where they will see some of the items that are on display at 221b Baker Street, such as Sherlock Holmes's Stradivarius violin and Dr. Watson's diary. Or they can read the biography of Sir Arthur Conan Doyle, which contains hyperlinks to information on Spiritualism and Ghosts on Film. They may read any of the Sherlock Holmes stories in e-text form, and they can view the original artwork accompanying these stories when they were first published. If they wish, students may listen to an actor's rendition of Holmes's lines, such as Sir Ralph Richardson stating of Professor Moriarty that "he is the Napoleon of crime. He is the organizer of half that is evil and of nearly all that is undetected in this great city." Truly committed Holmes fans may even wish to join one of the Sherlock Holmes societies around the world or to learn about the many stage, screen, television, and radio versions of the *Sherlock Holmes* stories. They may even read about the lives of actors, such as Basil Rathbone and Jeremy Brett, who have made Holmes so popular in film and television portrayals of the great detective.

Into the Wardrobe: The C. S. Lewis Web Site

http://www.ldscn.com/cslewis/main.shtml

Because the works of C. S. Lewis, such as *The Chronicles of Narnia,* are still protected by copyright, they are not yet available in e-text versions. Nevertheless, this site contains a very good annotated bibliography to help uninitiated readers determine which of Lewis's books they might wish to read. It even recommends the proper order in which to read the Narnia books. The site also contains interesting biographical essays and articles about Lewis's novels such as Matt Brennan's "The Lion, The Witch, and the Allegory: An Analysis of Selected Narnia Chronicles." Students may view here as well a map of Narnia and various beautiful images such as a painting of Aslan the lion.

George Orwell Homepage

http://www.k-1.com/Orwell/

If you are teaching *1984* or *Animal Farm,* you might find the interpretations of these novels that are provided on the *George Orwell Homepage* to be useful. The complete text of Orwell's essay, "Politics and the English Language," is available here and is a useful tool with which to help your students analyze the propaganda techniques practiced by Big Brother and Napoleon the pig in Orwell's novels. Your students might also find the biography of Orwell and some of his other essays to be useful in understanding his novels, and they might enjoy learning about some of Orwell's other books, such as *Burmese Days* and *Homage to Catalonia.* If they wish to share their ideas about his works they may join the Orwell Discussion Board.

AMERICAN AUTHORS

American Authors on the Web

http://lang.nagoya-u.ac.jp/~matsuoka/AmeLit.html

This amazing list of resources contains more than 1,000 links to information on American authors, from the popular contemporary writers such as Tom Clancy, Michael Crichton, and Anne Rice to the traditionally revered authors such as Edgar Allan Poe, Emily Dickinson, and Mark Twain. It is definitely a good place to begin your search for teaching ideas about American authors.

Literary Resources—American

http://andromeda.rutgers.edu/~jlynch/Lit/american.html

While this list of resources contains fewer links than the preceding one (less than 200), it differs from *American Authors on the Web* in that, as well as providing an excellent selection of author home pages, it also offers links to a number of overview sites, with titles such as 19th Century American Women Writers, The Mississippi Writers' Page, and Native American Literature Online. At the Beat poetry site, Literary Kicks, for instance, senior high school students can study the work of Jack Kerouac, Allen Ginsberg, and Lawrence Ferlinghetti. Or, if they visit the jazz literature archive site, Epistrophy, they will encounter an impressive collection of writings on literature and jazz, with introductions, samples of jazz fiction and poetry, and essays.

Author's Pen

http://www.books.com/scripts/authors.exe

Like the *American Authors on the Web* site, this *Author's Pen* page also contains links to approximately 1,000 home pages. But whereas the American Authors site lists its information chronologically according to the dates when the writers were born, the *Author's Pen* site lists its links in alphabetical order. Another difference between these two sites is that *American Authors on the Web* limits itself exclusively to American writers while the Author's Pen site includes some non-American authors such as Jane Austen and Thomas Hardy.

   If you are particularly interested in finding information on writers of children's and young adult literature, such as Ursula LeGuin and V. C. Andrews, then this *Author's Pen* site is the best of the three encyclopedic American writer's sites. Among the wide variety of American authors listed on this site are Ralph Ellison, the African-American writer of the novel, *Invisible Man,* Tony Hillerman, the writer of a series of Navajo detective novels such as *Skinwalkers,* and *Carson McCullers,* author of *The Heart Is a Lonely Hunter.*

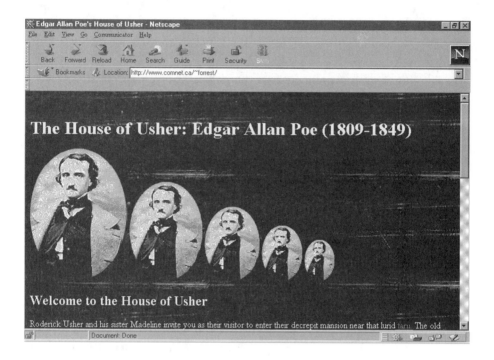

The House of Usher: Edgar Allan Poe (1809–1849)

http://www.comnet.ca/~forrest/

When your students first arrive at this delightfully macabre multimedia site they will encounter morbid, spine-tingling music and a bloodcurdling scream! They can then read a brief biography of Poe and, by visiting The Poe Decoder site, study some very helpful interpretations of his work. If they wish to see some of the houses where Poe and his 13-year-old wife lived, they can follow the Poe's Favorite Haunts link. If they wish to read e-texts of his works or study criticism about "The Black Cat," "The Raven," and many other stories and poems by Poe, they can proceed to The Poe Virtual Library. In the pages devoted to Poe's recurrent motifs and themes, your students will encounter animations of a beating heart and gnashing teeth. Through the Edgar Allan Poe Theatre's Real Audio feed they can listen to dramatizations of stories such as "The Mask of the Red Death." All of these imaginative features will undoubtedly delight many adolescent visitors.

Nathaniel Hawthorne

http://eldred.ne.mediaone.net/nh/hawthorne.html

If your students enjoy Poe's tales, then they might also enjoy many of Nathaniel Hawthorne's macabre stories such as "Young Goodman Brown" and "The Minister's

Black Veil." Hawthorne's complete works are now available on the Internet at the *Nathaniel Hawthorne* home page. Your students may also read here more than 20 different biographical accounts concerning, for instance, Hawthorne's relationships with other contemporary American authors such as Herman Melville and Henry David Thoreau. They can even read letters from Melville to Hawthorne and a diary entry by Hawthorne about Melville. There are more than 50 literary critical works on Hawthorne that they can study here, including three reviews by Edgar Allan Poe of Hawthorne's tales. Finally, this site contains links to a number of interesting related web pages such as the Discovery Channel's lesson plan on Hawthorne's novel *The Scarlet Letter.*

Emily Dickinson

http://www.planet.net/pkrisxle/emily/dickinson.html

The *Emily Dickinson* site contains links to over 470 of her poems as well as a number of short biographies. Included among the biographical pages is the Virtual Emily site, which provides visitors with many interesting pictures of Emily's relatives and of the homestead in Amherst where she lived as a recluse during the final years of her life. One photo is of a basket she used to fill with cookies and then lower on a rope to the village children in the garden below her bedroom window. The *Emily Dickinson* site also provides access to an audio file of actress Julie Harris reading a selection of Emily's poems and letters. There is even a recipe for Emily's Black Cake available and updated for modern kitchens.

Ever the Twain Shall Meet: Mark Twain on the Web

http://www.lm.com/~joseph/mtwain.html

This Mark Twain site contains links to electronic versions of many of his popular works as well as a collection of interesting quotations such as, "It is better to keep your mouth shut and appear stupid than to open it and remove all doubt."

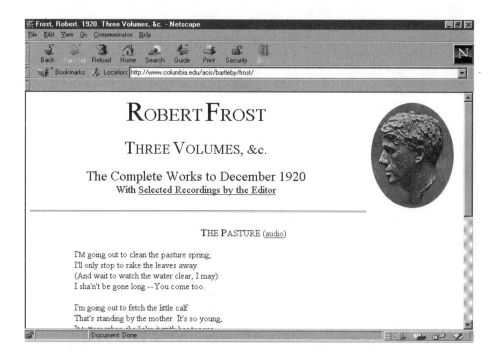

Robert Frost

http://www.columbia.edu/acis/bartleby/frost/

At this site your students can read those poems that were published by Robert Frost before 1920, and they can listen to audio files of some of his more well-known poems such as "Mending Wall" and "The Road Not Taken."

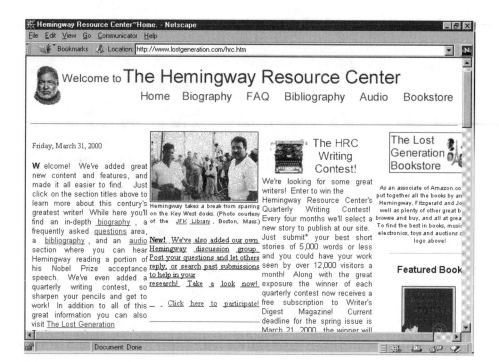

The Hemingway Resource Center

http://www.lostgeneration.com/hrc.htm

At the *Hemingway Resource Center* your students can find many photographs of Ernest Hemingway taken during his years as a writer, soldier, and hunter. Students can read answers to a list of FAQs about the author such as, "What characterizes Hemingway's writing style?" and they can listen to an audio file of Hemingway reading his Nobel Prize acceptance speech. Also available at this site are an illustrated six-part biography of Hemingway and a bibliography of books by and about Hemingway. Some of the many links that this site provides to other Hemingway pages are *Hemingway's Birthplace, The Running of the Bulls,* and *The Hemingway Cookbook.*

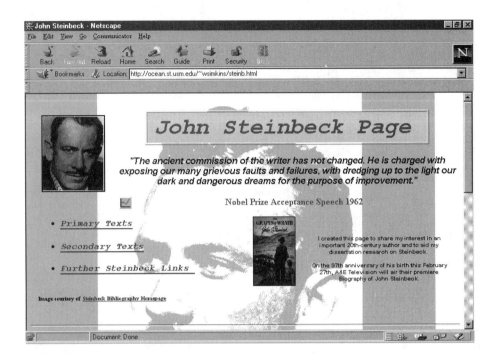

John Steinbeck Page

http://ocean.st.usm.edu/~wsimkins/steinb.html

A few of John Steinbeck's writings are available through this site, such as his essays from America and Americans and a selection of his letters from *Steinbeck: A Life in Letters.* But the most valuable feature of this site for teachers and students of Steinbeck's work is an extensive annotated bibliography of criticism written about his books. One of the related sites to which this one is linked is the *Of Mice and Men Student Survival Guide,* which provides hyperlinked definitions of words, references for allusions, and explanations of idioms for each chapter of this popular Steinbeck novel.

The Mississippi Writers Page: Tennessee Williams

http://www.olemiss.edu/depts/english/ms-writers/dir/williams_tennessee/

At this Tenessee Williams site your students may view a number of photographs of Williams at various stages in his career. This web page also contains a biography of Tennesse Williams as well as excellent summaries of a few of his more famous plays, such as *A Streetcar Named Desire.* One of this site's related links will take your students to a page devoted to Williams' play *The Glass Menagerie,* where they can read biographical, feminist, and psychoanalytic critical analyses, listen to audio clips, and view video clips of the play.

Crucible Home Page

http://www.geocities.com/CollegePark/Classroom/3085/crucible.html

There are many excellent links from this site to specific aspects of Arthur Miller's play, *The Crucible*. The first link takes you to *A Teacher's Cyberguide* for the play, which contains interesting teaching activities. For instance, students are asked to write a persuasive letter to the governor of Salem calling for action against the trials or to compose a tribute to the accused. They learn about the setting and the historical background of *The Crucible* and take a web tour of historical Salem, including a visit to the Witch Trials Memorial. They also read a chronology of the historical events of the witch trials. Another interesting link from *The Crucible* page provides an audio clip of the Anti-Communist American Senator Joe McCarthy, the person upon whom Miller based the character of Danforth.

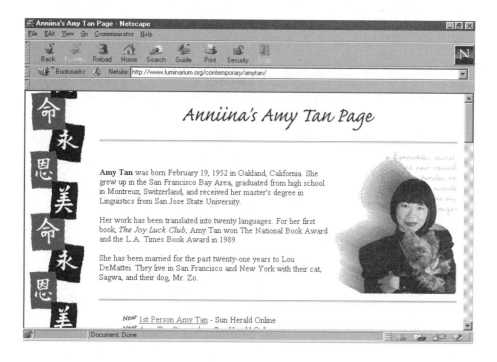

Anniina's Amy Tan Page

http://www.luminarium.org/contemporary/amytan/

Amy Tan's home page contains an illustrated version of one of her short stories, numerous reviews of her novels, and an enchanting audio clip of her account about her fascination with ghosts and with the enduring power of love. It also contains several biographical sketches of Amy Tan and links to a number of interesting essays with titles such as "Chinese-American Women in American Culture."

CANADIAN AUTHORS

Northwest Passages: Canadian Literature On-Line

http://www.nwpassages.com/nwplink.asp

This encyclopedic site connects to more than 200 Canadian authors' pages. It also contains many excellent links to web sites on Canadian Literature, Publishers, Periodicals, Organizations, Programs and Associations. It provides an extensive set of links as well to sites on African Canadian Literature, British Columbian Fiction Writers, Canadian Children's Books, Canadian Science Fiction, The Canadian Literature Discussion Group, Winners of the Stephen Leacock Medal for Humor, and Women in Canadian Literature.

Robertson Davies

http://starship.skyport.net/~amk/davies/

By the time Robertson Davies died at the age of 82 in 1995, his many novels, such as *Fifth Business,* had won him an honorary doctorate from Oxford University and the first honorary membership for a Canadian in the American Academy and Institute of Arts and Letters. This web page provides an overview of Davies's life and literary achievements. It also contains links to reviews of his novels and plays, interviews and photographs of the author, a selection of his famous quotations, and an e-mail discussion list that senior high school students and teachers might wish to join.

Margaret Atwood Information Site

http://www.cariboo.bc.ca/atwood/

The Atwood Society has created this *Margaret Atwood Information Site* to display for interested scholars lists of Atwood's novels, books of poetry, short stories, criticism, children's books, interviews, films, sound recordings, and dramatic works. This site also contains an extensive list of books about Margaret Atwood's life and works, such as the collection of essays titled *Approaches to Teaching Margaret Atwood's Handmaid's Tale and Other Works.* Among the Internet resources listed at this site is Margaret Atwood's own home page. The Atwood Society's page, however, is more extensive than Atwood's own site, so it is still the best place to start your search for resources on one of Canada's leading contemporary writers.

Michael Ondaatje Information

http://www.cariboo.bc.ca/ae/engml/FRIEDMAN/ondaatje.htm

Since the movie *The English Patient* won so many Academy Awards, most high school students will be familiar with the film based upon Michael Ondaatje's Booker Prize–winning novel. At this site they can learn more about the movie and book, the author's biography, and his other novels. One particularly valuable feature of this site is its lengthy and detailed index of words and phrases from *The English Patient,* which could prove useful to senior high school students should you choose to teach them the novel.

MULTICULTURAL AND WORLD LITERATURE AUTHORS

Voice of the Shuttle: English Literature: Minority Literatures

http://humanitas.ucsb.edu/shuttle/eng-min.html

This web page contains a large and excellent selection of links to Afro-American, Asian-American, Chicano, Jewish, and Native-American literature sites. Through the *Voice of the Shuttle,* for instance, your students can find their way to web pages on the life and works of such African-American writers as Maya Angelou, Ralph Ellison, Langston Hughes, Alice Walker, and Richard Wright.

Native American Authors
http://www.ipl.org/ref/native/

For students and teachers who would like to discover information about Canadian and American First Nations authors, the *Native American Authors* site contains a list of 400 writers in which can be found brief biographies and detailed catalogues of the 700 books they have written. Here students can read, for example, about the lives and works of Canadian First Nations writers such as Rita Joe, Tomson Highway, and Ruby Slipperjack or American First Nations authors N. Scott Momaday, James Welch, and Paula Gunn Allen.

The Index of Native American Electronic Text Resources
http://www.hanksville.org/NAresources/indices/NAetext.html

The *Index of Native American Electronic Text Resources* on the Internet contains many contemporary and historical essays, poems, and short stories by Canadian and American writers. For instance, Thomas King's essay, "Shooting the Lone Ranger," and Leslie Marmon Silko's essay, "Fences Against Freedom," are available online through this extensive index.

Literary Resources—Other National Literatures
http://andromeda.rutgers.edu/~jlynch/Lit/other.html

Some of the many countries whose literatures are represented on this site in English or English translation are Australia, New Zealand, France, Germany, India, Ireland, Italy, Japan, Spain, and Turkey. Through the link to South Asian Women's Literature, for example, your students can learn about the lives and works of such famous South Asian writers as Anita Desai, Ruth Prawar Jhabvala, and Mahasweta Devi. Or, through the Literature of South Asia and the Indian Diaspora site, they can explore a large assortment of links to learn about the works of writers such as Salman Rushdie, Rohinton Mistry, and R. K. Narayan.

Lu Xun
http://www-hsc.edu/~gallaher/luxun/luxun.html

When your students go to the site of the famous Chinese writer of the 1920s, Lu Xun, as well as viewing portraits of the author and reading his biography, they can study in English translation several of his short stories, such as "The Madman's Diary" and "A Small Incident." And if you have any students in your class who can read Chinese, they will be happy to see that the site offers Chinese versions of Lu Xun's works as well.

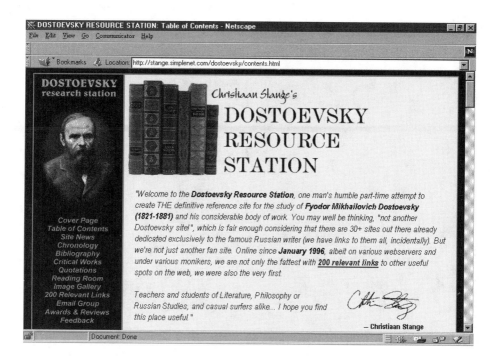

Dostoevsky Resource Station

http://stange.simplenet.com/dostoevsky/contents.html

As well as providing e-texts for all of Dostoevsky's novels, this site contains links to 200 other relevant sites with titles such as "Critical Essays," "Artwork Inspired by Dostoevsky," and "Study Guides and Plot Outlines." The site also offers opportunites to join several different discussion groups and mailing lists. Following are two of the questions students are asked to consider, for example, in the extensive study guide for Dostoevsky's novel *Crime and Punishment:* (1) Delineate the "superior man" argument, and evaluate Raskolnikov by the theory. (2) Consider the different dreams throughout the novel, and decide what functional role they fulfill.

Kazuo Ishiguro

http://www.stg.brown.edu/projects/hypertext/landow/post/uk/ishiguro/ishig uroov.html

Kazuo Ishiguro moved to England when he was six years old and grew up straddling two societies, the Japan of his parents and his adopted England. This site about the author of the award-winning novels *The Remains of the Day* and *Pale View of Hills* contains many interesting essays about Ishiguro's narrative technique, his themes of honesty and deception, his use of language and imagery, and many other topics.

SUGGESTED ACTIVITIES

1. Visit the *Children's Literature Web Guide* and some of the other major children's literature sites that are linked to it, such as Carol Hurst's site and Kay Vander-grift's. With your school librarian and/or your fellow language arts teachers, se-lect a number of author pages and then construct theme units around clusters of their works. For instance, under the theme of "perilous journeys" you could in-clude sites about the *Wizard of Oz* and *Alice in Wonderland.*

2. Encourage your adolescent students to visit the sites of authors whose works they have been studying, such as Gary Paulsen or S.E. Hinton, and to report to the class what they have learned about the authors' biographies and related works. If

a particular site provides an opportunity to contact the author, they could also be encouraged to send an e-mail in which they ask questions about the author's life and works.

3. For students who have an interest in science fiction, you could ask them to visit a site about one of their favorite authors and do one of the following: (1) read a few of the linked essays about the author's books and write a brief summary of their main arguments, or (2) view and critique some of the artwork inspired by the author's books and then draw their own picture based upon one of their favorite scenes.

4. While your students are reading stories from several mythology sites, encourage them to compare the archetypal patterns in myths from different cultures (heroes, quests, monsters, morals, etc.).

5. Have your students select and print out from different sites a number of their favorite poems (written by students or professional authors) about a common theme such as love or the seasons, then write, illustrate, and tape record one of their own poems about the same theme. Finally, have them post their poem on an Internet site such as Poetry Pals.

6. Find a lesson plan from a site such as EducETH about a novel which you teach and adapt that plan to suit the needs of your students.

7. In connection with a theme your students are studying, encourage them to visit the Improv Page and to perform several of the improvisations described at this site. Or download scripts from the Dramatic Exchange site that deal with this theme and have your students perform them.

8. From the assortment of British, American, Canadian, multicultural, and world literature author sites provided in this chapter, have each of your secondary school students select a different author for an independent study project.

SUMMARY

In this chapter we have introduced you to a wide range of literature sites that contain, for example, critical essays, audio clips of poetry readings, author biographies, and interactive lesson plans. Artwork, student writing, and film critiques are also included here. All of these resources can expand your repertoire beyond the usual options for teaching literature appreciation. Even though we have barely scratched the surface, we hope that this chapter has helped you to recognize the potential of these literature sites.

CHAPTER 5

Language Arts Standards and Activities

- English Language Arts Standards
- Researching the History of English Literature
- Grammar Online
- Publishing and Exploring Student Writing
- Writing Newspapers and Magazines
- Debating and Speech Writing
- Composing and Sharing Multimedia Presentations
- English-as-a-Second-Language (ESL) Projects and Resources
- Intercultural Communication Via E-mail
- Comparing Other Languages with English
- Creating School Home Pages
- Newspapers and Magazines
- Film

ENGLISH LANGUAGE ARTS STANDARDS

In 1996 the International Reading Association (IRA) and the National Council of Teachers of English (NCTE) established a set of standards for the study of English in their document, *Standards for the English Language Arts* (**http://www.ncte.org/standards/thelist.html**). In this chapter we have identified a number of sites you may find useful for enabling your students to achieve these various literacy standards. For instance, one of the NCTE standards is for students to be able to "read a wide range of print and nonprint texts to build an understanding of texts, of themselves, and of the cultures of the United States and the world." To help your students to develop their print and media literacy skills, therefore, we have described how you can use a number of newspaper, magazine, and film sites to show your students how to understand events and ideas in their country and their world.

Another important NCTE standard is for your students to be able to "read a wide range of literature from many periods in many genres to build an understanding of the many dimensions of human experience." At the end of the previous chapter we showed you some of the splendid multicultural and world literature sites available for elementary and secondary school students to visit, but in this chapter we also present some Internet pages that are devoted to the history of English literature so that you can aid young readers to view human experience through the eyes of some of the England's finest writers. A related standard is to be able to "apply a wide range of strategies to comprehend, interpret, evaluate, and appreciate texts," so in this section on reseaching the history of English literature, we begin by providing you with an excellent literary criticism site.

Three standards that concern how to teach students to become more effective writers are to "adjust their use of spoken, written, and visual language to communicate effectively with a variety of audiences and for different purposes, to employ a wide range of strategies as they write and use different writing process elements appropriately to communicate with different audiences for a variety of purposes, and to participate as knowledgeable, reflective, creative, and critical members of a variety of literacy communities." So that you may enable your students to achieve these three standards, we provide a number of sites under the headings of "Publishing and Exploring Student Writing" and "Writing Newspapers and Magazines" that show how to write well and how to publish work on the Internet.

Concerning your students' need to be able to "apply knowledge of language structure, language conventions, media techniques, figurative language, and genre to create, critique, and discuss print and nonprint texts," we have brought together in this chapter a number of pages devoted to helping your students with grammar and to showing them how to compose and share multimedia presentations. And our sections on intercultural communication via email, comparing other languages with English, and creating school home pages will help your students to realize their potential to "(1) conduct research on issues and interests by generating ideas and questions and by posing problems; (2) develop an understanding and respect for diversity and language use, patterns, and dialects across cultures, ethnic groups, geographic regions, and social roles; and (3) use a variety of technological and informational resources to gather and synthesize information to create and communicate knowledge."

Finally, in this chapter we have selected some very good ESL project and resource pages to help your elementary and secondary school ESL students achieve the NCTE standard of "making use of their first language to develop competency in English language arts and develop understanding across the curriculum." And for all of your students who need to learn how to "use spoken, written, and visual language to accomplish their own purposes (learning, enjoyment, persuasion, and exchange of information," the debating and speech writing sites assembled here should help them to improve their powers of persuasion in speaking and writing.

In this chapter, then, we ask you to bear in mind these NCTE standards for the study of English language arts so that you can see how particular sites may help you to guide your students toward the achievement of each of the learning outcomes just delineated.

RESEARCHING THE HISTORY OF ENGLISH LITERATURE

When you are teaching students about the history of English literature, the following sites will enable you to show them the writings of different authors over the centuries. The first site provides an overview of British and American literature and literary criticism from the fourteenth century to the present. The subsequent sites enable you to focus on particular eras by viewing orginal manuscripts and listening to audioclips of the works of Chaucer and others.

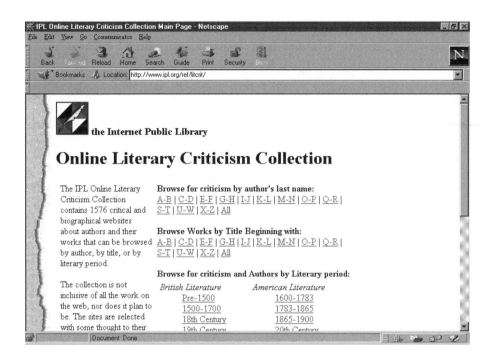

Online Literary Criticism Collection

http://www.ipl.org/ref/litcrit/	
Intended Audience	Students and teachers
Grade Level	9-12
Curricular Fit	English language study and Old English Literature
Types of Resources	Lists of Literary Critical and author websites
Authorship of Site	The Internet Public Library
Navigation	Good
Visual Appeal	Good
Interactive Activity	None

The Online Literary Criticism Collection site provides an incredibly large collection of links to sites such as *The English Language in the Fourteenth Century,* which describes the changes that took place in the Engish language during the fourteenth century by focusing particularly upon the language used in *The Canterbury Tales* and how that reflected the dialects of Chaucer's times. As well as critical and linguistic sites, this page can connect you to home pages and biographical information about many of the most famous British and American writers.

Resources for Studying Beowulf

http://www.georgetown.edu/irvinemj/english016/beowulf/beowulf.html	
Intended Audience	Students and teachers
Grade Level	9-12
Curricular Fit	English language study and Old English Literature
Types of Resources	Original and two translations of poem. Learning old English.
Authorship of Site	Martin Irvine & Deborah Everhart at Georgetown University
Navigation	Good.
Visual Appeal	Good. Can view original manuscript.
Interactive Activity	Some (Key word search of poem possible)

This site and the next one are both part of Georgetown University's *The Labyrinth: Resources for Medieval Studies,* a wonderful collection of materials for the study of Medieval English literature and culture. Here students can view fragments of the poem from an original manuscript, or they can compare the Old English version of *Beowulf* with two translations.

Labyrinth Library: Middle English Bookcase

http://www.georgetown.edu/labyrinth/library/me/me.html	
Intended Audience	Students and teachers
Grade Level	9-12
Curricular Fit	English language study and Middle English Literature
Types of Resources	Electronic texts of Chaucer's Canterbury Tales and others.
Authorship of Site	Martin Irvine & Deborah Everhart at Georgetown University
Navigation	Good
Visual Appeal	Good
Interactive Activity	None

This site contains the complete texts of many famous Middle English works such as *Sir Gawain and the Green Knight, Everyman, The Vision of Piers Plowman,* and *The Canterbury Tales.* It also has links to other anthologies and collections of Medieval Literature in which students can hear Middle English being spoken.

The Edmund Spenser Home Page

http://darkwing.uoregon.edu/~rbear/	
Intended Audience	Student and teachers
Grade Level	11-12
Curricular Fit	English language study and Renaissance English Literature
Types of Resources	Electronic texts, discussion list achive, critical essays
Authorship of Site	Richard Bear at the University of Oregon
Navigation	Good
Visual Appeal	Good
Interactive Activity	Some if students choose to join discussion list

The life and works of Edmund Spenser, author of *The Faerie Queene*, are celebrated in this rich site that contains electronic versions of his complete works. Your students can read critical essays about Spencer's poetry or read archived discussions among Spencer scholars.

The Milton-L Home Page

http://www.urich.edu/~creamer/milton/	
Intended Audience	Students, teachers, and professors
Grade Level	11-12
Curricular Fit	English language study and 17th Century English Literature
Types of Resources	Essays, e-texts, audio clips of poetry, discussion lists
Authorship of Site	
Navigation	Good
Visual Appeal	Excellent
Interactive Activity	Viewing paintings and listening to poetry

The complete electronic text of Milton's *Paradise Lost* is available through this site, as are audio files of the arguments for each of the twelve books of that famous epic poem. Students can study *A John Milton Chronology*, view wonderful illustrations of his poetry, and read reviews of recently published books about the life and works of Milton.

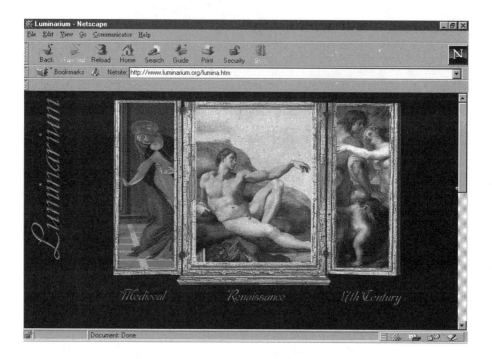

Luminarium: Medieval, Renaissance, and 17th Century Literary Anthologies

http://www.luminarium.org/lumina.htm	
Intended Audience	Students and teachers
Grade Level	9-12
Curricular Fit	English language study, 15th through 17th Century Literature
Types of Resources	Paintings, music and poetry audio files, e-texts, critical essays
Authorship of Site	Luminarium
Navigation	Good
Visual Appeal	Excellent
Interactive Activity	Listening to poetry and music and viewing illustrations

At the *Luminarium Medieval, Renaissance, and 17th Century English Literature* sites, your students can study ancient manuscripts, listen to portions of Chaucer's *Canterbury Tales* being read, or view the original title page of Christopher Marlowe's

Dr. Faustus. There is a wonderful collection of essays at each site with which your students could carry out independent study projects. The sites' index pages even provide medieval and Renaissance music clips for your students' listening pleasure. This is an exceptionally well-presented and interesting set of sites.

GRAMMAR ONLINE

Online English Grammar

http://www.edunet.com/english/grammar/index.html	
Intended Audience	Students
Grade Level	7-12
Curricular Fit	Grammar and writing process
Types of Resources	Example sentences and grammatical explanations
Authorship of Site	Anthony Hughes
Navigation	Good
Visual Appeal	Fair
Interactive Activity	None

The *Online English Grammar* site is valuable first of all because it can provide your students with an alphabetical list of descriptions of all of the basic grammatical structures and parts of speech you would like them to master as they create and revise their own writing. But this site also contains links to other useful gammar sites, such as the *English Grammar Clinic,* where once your students register they can receive help with their grammatical problems.

Guide to Grammar and Writing

http://webster.commnet.edu/HP/pages/darling/original.htm	
Intended Audience	Students
Grade Level	7-12
Curricular Fit	Grammar and writing process
Types of Resources	Descriptions of sentence, paragraph, and essay types
Authorship of Site	Charles Darling
Navigation	Good
Visual Appeal	Good
Interactive Activity	Questions can be asked of Gramma(r) English

At the *Guide to Grammar and Writing* site, information is available about sentence, paragraph, and essay forms. Your students can click on a picture of Gramma(r) English in her rocking chair in order to submit a question to her about a particular grammar problem they are having. There are also several other interesting features to this site, such as the humorous grammar errors listed in the *Anomalous Anonymies* page. Some of the other activities listed here include

■ Models for communication
■ Interactive quizzes
■ Grammar logs
■ Eminent quotables
■ Other online resources for writing

PUBLISHING AND EXPLORING STUDENT WRITING

Positively Poetry

http://advicom.net/~e-media/kv/poetry1.html	
Intended Audience	Young poets
Grade Level	5-10
Curricular Fit	Creative writing
Types of Resources	List of writing topics, students' poems from many countries
Authorship of Site	Kellie Vaughn
Navigation	Good
Visual Appeal	Fair
Interactive Activity	None

Positively Poetry is a site that illustrates both the strengths and weaknesses of the Internet's interactive and democratic features. Kellie Vaughn, a 15-year-old girl, constructed this site in 1995 to give young poets like herself ideas from which to write their own poems and a place in which to publish their work. By the summer of 1998 Kellie was forced to stop receiving new submissions because the numbers of poems she received each day was becoming overwhelming. We commend Kellie's efforts and still recommend this site as a place were your students can find good poetry topics and can read other students work.

In the following sites you will see opporunities to read and publish student work as well as aids to the writing process. We suggest that as well as considering these sites as venues for your students' work, you consider publishing their poems and short stories on your school's home page so that when children and teachers from other schools come to your school's site they will quickly derive a sense of the people and place they are visiting. The next site, *Our Poetry Imaginations: Mrs. Jones' Second Grade Poetry Collection,* illustrates this point.

Our Poetry Imaginations: Mrs. Jones' Second Grade Poetry Collection

http://www.frii.com/~darhodes/	
Intended Audience	Teachers and students
Grade Level	2 and higher
Curricular Fit	Creative writing and theme units
Types of Resources	Poems, pictures, and writing strategies
Authorship of Site	J. Elder and D. Rhodes
Navigation	Good
Visual Appeal	Good
Interactive Activity	None

This delightful poetry page illustrates how to enable a class of grade 2 students to compose free-verse poems by going through a four-step composition process. First the students here carried out research on various birds. Then they brainstormed lists of the birds' characteristics and from these created the poems and drawings that they published on the Internet. The resultant compositions are remarkably good.

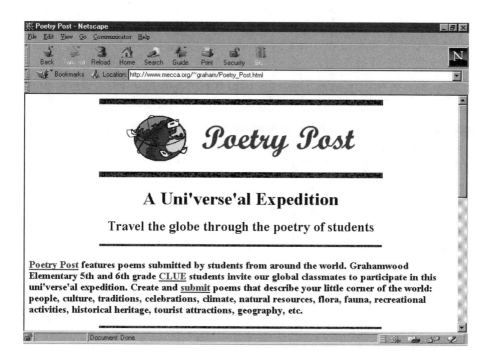

Poetry Post

http://www.mecca.org/~graham/Poetry_Post.html	
Intended Audience	Teachers and students
Grade Level	5-8
Curricular Fit	Creative writing and multicultural theme units
Types of Resources	Poems, cultural background information, e-mail addresses
Authorship of Site	Grahamwood Elementary School grade 5 and 6 students
Navigation	Good (although some links do not work)
Visual Appeal	Good
Interactive Activity	Reading poems and cultural info, then adding own poems

Grahamwood Elementary School's grade 5 and 6 gifted students have created a site at which visitors can read poems from students around the world and then post their own poems to add to the collection. Young authors are encouraged to write about the people, culture, traditions, and geography of their regions. The site therefore provides a global, multicultural perspective on poetry reading and writing. It also contains links to information about the countries of the contributing students from Israel and Australia and the e-mail addresses of these young poets.

Roget's Thesaurus

http://web.cs.city.ac.uk/text/roget/thesaurus.html	
Intended Audience	Teachers and students
Grade Level	3-12
Curricular Fit	Writing process
Types of Resources	Word search for synonyms
Authorship of Site	MICRA, Inc.
Navigation	Good
Visual Appeal	Fair
Interactive Activity	Limited to the usual thesaurus functions

If your students are looking for just the right word to use in their poems and short stories, this site offers them an excellent opportunity to search *Roget's Thesaurus* for an extensive set of synonyms. Two other sites young wordsmiths should visit are *The Semantic Ryming Dictionary* (**http://www.link.cs.cmu.edu/dougb/rhyme-doc.html**) and the *WWWebster Dictionary* site (**http://www.m-w.com/dictionary**).

Inkspot.com: The Writer's Resource For Young Writers

http://www.inkspot.com/joe/young/	
Intended Audience	Adolescent writers
Grade Level	7-12
Curricular Fit	Creative writing
Types of Resources	Discussion forums, posted stories and poems, articles
Authorship of Site	Joe Holler
Navigation	Good
Visual Appeal	Fair
Interactive Activity	The forums, articles, and posted works are quite engaging

Inkspot's Writer's Resource for Young Writers contains interesting opportunities for adolescents to discuss in e-mail lists the writing ideas and approaches that are of interest to them. They can also attempt to publish their work at this site, although obviously very few works are accepted for publication here, and they can read articles by professional writers about their craft. There are also links to classified adds that can tell them where to publish their work professionally, either in paper form or online. In Inkspot's related *Writing Genre's* page students can learn how to write mysteries, science fiction, drama, children's books, horror, and romance short stories and novels.

The Biography Maker

http://www.bham.wednet.edu/bio/biomaker.htm	
Intended Audience	Students
Grade Level	4-12
Curricular Fit	Biographical writing in theme units
Types of Resources	Lists of biographies, tips for research and writing
Authorship of Site	Bellingham Schools
Navigation	Good
Visual Appeal	Fair
Interactive Activity	The Biography Maker works like a machine

This ingenious site gives students all the tools they need in order to write interesting biographies. The students are encouraged to begin by raising important questions about the person they are studying. Then they are asked to look for information about that person in books, electronic encyclopedias, and Internet sites. Finally, they are shown how to synthesize their material and organize their writing so that they can tell a good story. Links to lists of biographies are also provided as examples for students to read.

The Eclectic Writer

http://www.eclectics.com/writing/writing.html	
Intended Audience	Students
Grade Level	10-12
Curricular Fit	Writer's workshop
Types of Resources	Essays about writing
Authorship of Site	
Navigation	Good
Visual Appeal	Good
Interactive Activity	Mainly a valuable resource page

Although this site was created with adult authors in mind, it can serve equally well as a resource for serious adolescent authors in writing courses or in your high school's writing club. *The Eclectic Writer* contains an extensive list of sites organized under the following categories:

■ Web-based discussion board for writers

■ Articles about writing

■ Fiction writers' character chart

■ Crime writing

■ Romance writing

■ Horror writing

■ Children's writing

■ Technical writing

■ Screen writing

■ Science fiction/fantasy writing

■ Mystery writing

■ Poetry

■ Newsgroups

■ Research

■ General writing resources

■ Just for fun

WRITING NEWSPAPERS AND MAGAZINES

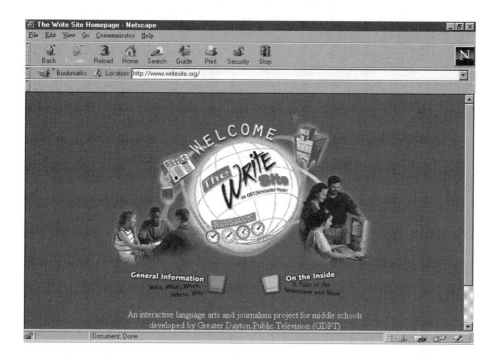

The Write Site

http://www.writesite.org/	
Intended Audience	Teachers and students
Grade Level	6-8
Curricular Fit	Creative writing and journalism
Types of Resources	Contains many newspaper writing resources and units
Authorship of Site	Greater Dayton Public Television
Navigation	Good
Visual Appeal	Good
Interactive Activity	Some related sites such as CNN provide video and audio

As the authors of *The Write Site* point out, middle school students who visit this multimedia language arts web page can learn how to enjoy the art of telling stories.

Students assume the roles of journalists who generate leads, gather facts, and write stories by using the tools and techniques of professional journalists. Within *The Write Site's Newsroom Page* for students are sections containing valuable links to help students write their stories.

The *Features Desk* contains links to

- The Story of Journalism in the United States
- Creating Human Interest
- Tapping News Organizations
- Cool Sites for Kids

The *Research Beat* links include

- How to Do Research
- Finding Data on the Internet
- Museums and Online Libraries

And the *Style Section* links include

- Developing Your Style
- Keeping a Journal
- Writers' Thoughts on Writing

For teachers, *The Write Site* contains four units of activities to be done with students:

- How the Newspaper Works
- A Day in the Life of a Reporter
- Newspapers in Cyberspace
- Let the Pictures Tell the Story

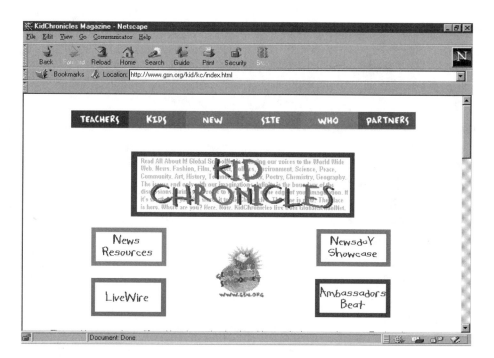

Kid Chronicles

http://www.gsn.org/kid/kc/index.html	
Intended Audience	Teachers and Students
Grade Level	4-12
Curricular Fit	Journalism and writing
Types of Resources	News resources, global current events by students
Authorship of Site	Global SchoolNet
Navigation	Good
Visual Appeal	Good
Interactive Activity	Opportunities to showcase your students' work globally

Like *The Write Site, Kid Chronicles* provides opportunities for your students to reseach, write, and share their news stories with other students on the Internet. Under the categories of News Resources, Live Wire, Newsday Showcase, and Ambassador's Beat, your students can research stories, read articles and editorials about current world events written by young people around the globe, and share individual or class projects with other visitors to this Global SchoolNet site.

DEBATING AND SPEECH WRITING

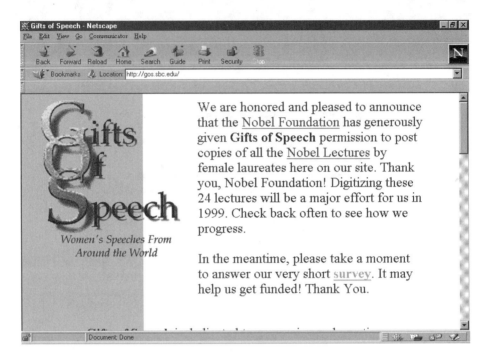

Gifts of Speech

http://gos.sbc.edu/	
Intended Audience	Students
Grade Level	10-12
Curricular Fit	Arguing from a position in written and spoken forms
Types of Resources	Large archive of famous women's speeches
Authorship of Site	Liz Linton and Tom Solomon
Navigation	Good
Visual Appeal	Good
Interactive Activity	None

Although there are many sites on the Internet devoted to debating and speech writing, if you are looking for a repository of wonderful model speeches by famous women, then the *Gifts of Speech* site is the best place to start. Among the many speeches available at this site are the 1991 Nobel Lecture on "Writing and Being" by

South African writer Nadine Gordimer and the speech on "The Problem of Racism on the Threshold of the 21st Century" by Guatemalan human rights activist, Rigoberta Menchu Tum.

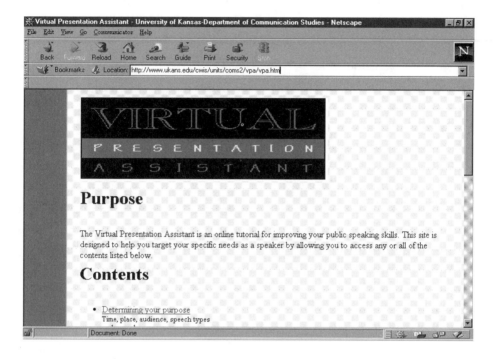

Virtual Presentation Assistant

http://www.ukans.edu/cwis/units/coms2/vpa/vpa.htm	
Intended Audience	Students and teachers
Grade Level	8-12
Curricular Fit	Speech writing and presenting
Types of Resources	Links to information on various aspects of speech making
Authorship of Site	Diana Carlin and James Payne at the University of Kansas
Navigation	Good
Visual Appeal	Fair
Interactive Activity	None

The *Virtual Presentation Assistant* page can provide your students with many helpful links to sites and suggestions about speech making. Under the title Researching Your Topic, for instance, are links to news resources, government and university libraries, and the *American Communication Reference Resources,* as well as advice on gathering information through interviews. Some of the other topics covered at this site are

- Determining your purpose
- Selecting your topic
- Analyzing your audience
- Supporting your points
- Outlining your points
- Using visual aids
- Presenting your speech
- Public speaking links

COMPOSING AND SHARING MULTIMEDIA PRESENTATIONS

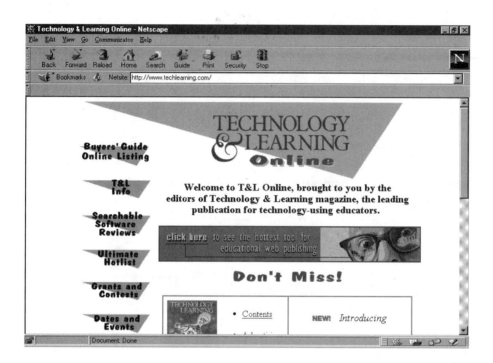

Technology and Learning Online

http://www.techlearning.com/	
Intended Audience	Teachers
Grade Level	K-12
Curricular Fit	Technological background information for teachers
Types of Resources	Software reviews, school website building tools
Authorship of Site	Technology and Learning Magazine
Navigation	Good
Visual Appeal	Good
Interactive Activity	None

If you would like to construct a website for your class or school in order to establish projects with other schools, or to publish your students writing assignments and multimedia Web projects on the Internet, then the home page produced by the editors of *Technology and Learning* magazine has much to offer. Reviews of more than 300 samples of English language arts software are available, as well as interviews with many leading experts on technology in schools. The following topics are explored in very infomative hyperlinked articles about how to build your own website.

- Why in the World Wide Web (Should We Build a Site of Our Own)?
- Housing Your Site
- Effective Site Design
- GUI/RUI
- Graphics
- Spreading the Word

ENGLISH-AS-A-SECOND-LANGUAGE (ESL) PROJECTS AND RESOURCES

The Internet for ESL Teachers

http://edvista.com/claire/internet-esl.html	
Intended Audience	Teachers of ESL
Grade Level	All grades
Curricular Fit	ESL
Types of Resources	Many valuable links to ESL-related sites, teacher guidelines
Authorship of Site	Claire Bradin
Navigation	Good
Visual Appeal	Fair
Interactive Activity	MOOs, intercultural e-mail communication

From this page you can go to the Michigan State University ESL Student Project page to view some of the interesting projects that ESL students at MSU have produced, such as geographical reports, information about their experiences of culture shock, examples of their toughest grammar problems and solutions, and advice to new ESL students. Or you can enter a MOO for ESL students through the link to schMOOze University, which is a site on the Internet established in 1994 to provide people studying English as a second or foreign language with opportunities to practice English while they share ideas and experiences. Although schMOOze University, was originally intended for the use of ESL/EFL students, it welcomes all people interested in cross-cultural communication.

If you are interested in creating your own ESL web page, the *Internet for ESL Teachers* home page provides, for example, a link to *Language Interactive,* a guide to web scripting for language learning. In its Dark Side of the Internet section, the *Internet for ESL Teachers* site introduces you to some of the more disturbing places that you should be aware of on the World Wide Web, such as the School Sucks site, where your students can download prewritten or customized essays instead of doing the writing themselves.

Linguistic Funland!

http://www.linguistic-funland.com/tesl-student-projects.html	
Intended Audience	Teachers and students of ESL
Grade Level	All grades
Curricular Fit	ESL
Types of Resources	Links to various worthwhile ESL project sites
Authorship of Site	Kristina Harris
Navigation	Good
Visual Appeal	Fair
Interactive Activity	ESL students can publish writing and read works by others

At *Linguistic Funland!* you and your students can find many interesting project ideas. Links are provided to sites about journal writing, English essays by Japanese students, a phrase pool, academic reading, and creative writing. Through the link to the *HUT International Writing Project* students can find writing topics such as taboos in specific cultures, how bilingualism affects people, and a memorable experience with a person from another culture.

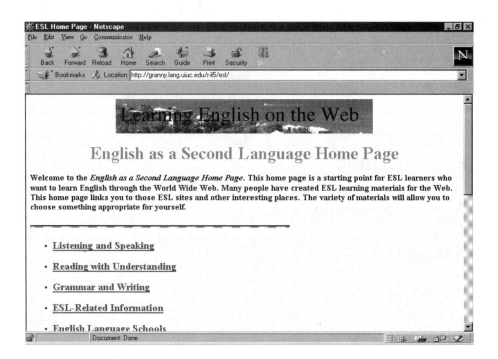

Learning English on the Web

http://granny.lang.uiuc.edu/r-li5/esl/	
Intended Audience	Teachers and students of ESL
Grade Level	All grades
Curricular Fit	ESL
Types of Resources	Links to useful ESL sites
Authorship of Site	Rong-Chang Li
Navigation	Good
Visual Appeal	Fair
Interactive Activity	ESL language listening labs and radio programs

At *Learning English on the Web* there are links to several different ESL Jobs sites where you can look for ESL teaching opportunities for yourself around the globe. Or you can access through the *New York Times* Daily Lesson Plans list a wonderful collection of illustrated articles and accompanying lesson plans for your students. This site also contains links to radio programs and a language listening lab.

INTERCULTURAL COMMUNICATION VIA E-MAIL

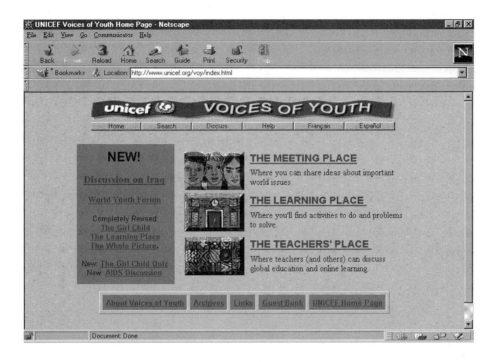

Voices of Youth

http://www.unicef.org/voy/index.html	
Intended Audience	Teachers and students
Grade Level	K-12
Curricular Fit	Reading and writing, intercultural communication, debate
Types of Resources	Classroom collaborative projects, teacher discussions
Authorship of Site	Unicef
Navigation	Good
Visual Appeal	Good
Interactive Activity	Students can write to each other about human rights issues

In the *Voices of Youth* site children from around the world are encouraged by UNICEF to share with each other through live chats and e-mail messages their views about such global human rights issues such as child labor, children in cities, and children in war. One of the particularly ingenious multimedia interactive features of the site is the activity called The Whole Picture, in which students are shown a portion of a picture and asked to guess what the rest of the picture contains. In one picture, for instance, a boy is shown cringing while he looks away from the source of his fear. When the students click on the blank portion of the picture they see that the boy is in fact in a health clinic receiving a vaccination. The *Voices of Youth* site provides excellent opportunities for your students to learn about the issues important to their peers in other countries by talking to them directly about these issues.

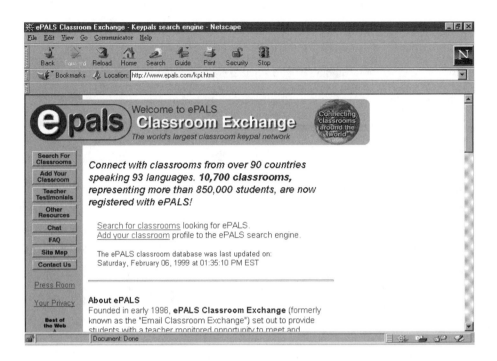

Epals Classroom Exchange

http://www.epals.com/kpi.html	
Intended Audience	Teachers and students
Grade Level	K-12
Curricular Fit	ESL, global issues theme units
Types of Resources	Lists of teachers and classes by subject, grade and country
Authorship of Site	Epals Classroom Exchange
Navigation	Good
Visual Appeal	Fair
Interactive Activity	Email intercultural exhanges

The *Epals* site has linked more than 750,000 students in 10,000 classrooms across 90 countries so that students can learn to express themselves across cultures by communicating with each other via the Internet. You can use the Epal search engine to look for partners by country or city, classroom grade or age, or you can list your own school at the Epals site and wait for another teacher to find you first. This is a wonderful and efficient way to connect your students to others around the globe.

The Electric Postcard

http://postcards.www.media.mit.edu/Postcards/Welcome.html	
Intended Audience	Teachers and students
Grade Level	K-12
Curricular Fit	Letter writing
Types of Resources	Various postcards that can be mailed electronically
Authorship of Site	Judith Donath at MIT Media Lab
Navigation	Good
Visual Appeal	Good
Interactive Activity	Choose your own postcards to post as email

Students can choose postcards to send by e-mail to their friends in other countries. These postcards can mark a holiday such as Hanukkah or Christmas, or they can highlight a certain artist's work such as Leonardo da Vinci or Paul Gauguin.

COMPARING OTHER LANGUAGES WITH ENGLISH

Travlang's Foreign Languages for Travelers

http://www.travlang.com/	
Intended Audience	Language learners of any age
Grade Level	K-12
Curricular Fit	Language study
Types of Resources	Sites for learning 70 languages, translators, dictionaries
Authorship of Site	Michael Martin, founder of Travlang
Navigation	Good
Visual Appeal	Good
Interactive Activity	Speaking, listening, and viewing of various languages

This site provides both rudimentary language instruction (by using audioclips of phrases and sentences) and more advanced language study (by providing links to sites with CDs, books, audiotapes, etc., that you can order for your class). It also provides electronic dictionaries that allow students to translate individual words instantly from one language into another. By studying how English differs from several other languages, you can give your students the opportunity to think more deeply about issues of linguistic and cultural translation. This site is particularly worthwhile if your students are reading stories and poems that have been translated into English from other languages, because you can consider what may have changed through the translation process.

Learn Chinese

http://pasture.ecn.purdue.edu/~agenhtml/agenmc/china/ctutor.html	
Intended Audience	Teachers and students of languages
Grade Level	4-12
Curricular Fit	Chinese language within a multicultural literature theme unit
Types of Resources	Chinese phrases in audio files
Authorship of Site	Haiwang Yuan and Remy Guo
Navigation	Good
Visual Appeal	Fair
Interactive Activity	Choice of many audioclips

This is just one of hundreds of sites you could visit with your students in order to provide them with an introduction to a variety of foreign languages. The extensive lists of audioclips available at this particular site are organized under the following categories: greetings, shopping, dining, travelling, and time.

CREATING SCHOOL HOME PAGES

```
Welcome - Netscape                                                    _ □ ×
File  Edit  View  Go  Communicator  Help

  Back   Forward  Reload  Home  Search  Guide  Print  Security  Stop          N

  Bookmarks   Location: http://www.netspace.net.au/~bansec/welcome.html

       Banksia Secondary College

    Thank you for visiting. The Web-Counter says that your lucky number is:  4301

       Who Are We?           Curriculum Areas          Facilities
       International Prospectus  The Deaf Facility      Dual Certification
       Multiculturalism       Extra-Curricular Activities  Maths Task Centre
       Vocational Pathways    The BIG Book  NEW         Newspaper articles
       Internet Projects      Star Students            Cyber Gallery
                              Farewell Mami

                    Please sign   [   ]   our guest book

          Cyber News                            Quicktime Movie!

                    G'day! - Welcome to Banksia Seco
```

Banksia Secondary College Home Page

http://www.netspace.net.au/~bansec/welcome.html	
Intended Audience	Teachers and students
Grade Level	8-12
Curricular Fit	Creative writing and intercultural communication
Types of Resources	Art, short stories, student biographies
Authorship of Site	Banksia School
Navigation	Good
Visual Appeal	Good
Interactive Activity	Travel with students on field trip, read creative writing

One way that you can help to make your school's presence known on the Internet is to develop a school home page that contains imaginative images and writing from your students. *The Banksia Secondary College Home Page* in Australia contains many interesting features that reflect the multicultural composition of the school. In a section titled the Banksia Big Book Archives, visiting students can read some of the best stories written each year by students from various grade levels in the school. In a letter to a racist Australian politician, for example, a Somalian refugee student states, "Who do you think you are? Does Australian politics allow this sort of behaviour in our country? Personally, I don't like racism, but you seem to be enjoying your new job promoting it." In another piece an Indonesian boy describes his escape from an erupting volcano before he moved to Australia. "Flaming boulders had tossed across the horizons and dropped down killing people before they had a chance to find shelter. The army couldn't help the survivors, because the black ashes covered the main road and made it very difficult for them to get into the remote areas. Few survived the disaster, I was one of them."

Some other imaginative ways in which Banksia's teachers use its home page to establish their students' identities on the Internet to are (1) exhibit their students' artwork in a Cyber Gallery; (2) highlight in a "Star Students" item the accomplishments and cultural backgrounds of their immigrant students from Somalia, Vietnam, Lebanon, China, the Philippines, Indonesia, Ethiopia, and sixteen other countries; (3) present photographic essays about school life such as the one in which the grade 7, 8, and 9 ESL students are shown making an excursion to a nearby wildlife sanctuary; and (4) describe in their Cyber News articles events such as the visit to their school of the Mayi Winba Dancers, an Aboriginal troupe from Northern Queensland.

Web66: International School Web Site Registry

http://web66.coled.umn.edu/schools.html	
Intended Audience	Teachers and students
Grade Level	K-12
Curricular Fit	Publishing home pages on the Internet
Types of Resources	Global list of elementary and secondary school home pages
Authorship of Site	Stephen E. Collins Web66 Webmaster
Navigation	Good
Visual Appeal	Good
Interactive Activity	Vast collection of links to schools worldwide

If you want to visit a number of school home pages in order to make connections with other teachers or to consider ways of making your own school's home page more interesting, you can use the *Web66 International School Web Site Registry,* which contains the home pages of thousands of schools around the world. Many of the middle and secondary school home pages that you can discover through this site contain information about each school's students and teachers such as their own individual home pages and e-mail addresses. Once you have found a school whose teachers and students might prove interesting partners for collaborative responses to world literature or cultural exchanges, you can send an e-mail to the teacher you have chosen and plan together possible activities between your classes.

NEWSPAPERS AND MAGAZINES

The Media Literacy Online Project

http://interact.uoregon.edu/MediaLit/HomePage	
Intended Audience	Teachers and students
Grade Level	6-12
Curricular Fit	Media literacy
Types of Resources	
Authorship of Site	College of Education, University of Oregon
Navigation	Good
Visual Appeal	Fair
Interactive Activity	None

The goal of the *Media Literacy Online Project* is to provide a support service for teachers, and others, concerned with the influence of media in the lives of children and youth. The site's authors have created this comprehensive media literacy resource collection to facilitate that objective. This extensive set of resources includes among its many links research into children and the media, media course syllabi, media guides (such as the PBS Teacher Resource), media museums, media production by and for children and youth, censorship, advertising, media violence, and on-line newspaper, magazine, music, radio, film and television services.

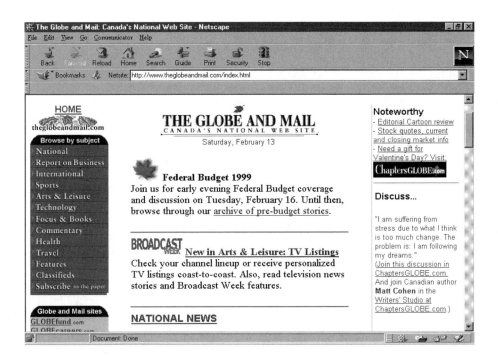

The Globe and Mail

http://www.theglobeandmail.com/index.html	
Intended Audience	Teachers and students
Grade Level	6-12
Curricular Fit	Newspapers in the classroom
Types of Resources	National and international news stories
Authorship of Site	*The Globe and Mail*
Navigation	Good
Visual Appeal	Good
Interactive Activity	None

The Globe and Mail is just one of hundreds of newspapers and magazines from around the world that are available via the Internet. Students can use newspaper sites such as these as models for their own newspaper writing activities; they can base their creative writing on the current events which they see recorded in these online newpapers; or they can sample a number of these papers from various countries to compare the opinions which they express about international stories. At *The Globe and Mail* site, for instance, they can read international and national news stories, business, sports, arts, and recreation items.

Voice of the Shuttle: Media Studies Page

http://humanitas.ucsb.edu/shuttle/media.html	
Intended Audience	Teachers and students
Grade Level	6-12
Curricular Fit	Media studies and journalism
Types of Resources	Newspapers, magazines, TV, film/video,radio, comics, CDs
Authorship of Site	Alan Liu
Navigation	Good
Visual Appeal	Good
Interactive Activity	Listening to radio broadcasts, reading newspapers

This site contains many excellent links to resources for the teaching of media literacy. Students can read Canadian, American, and international newspapers and magazines, or listen to radio broadcasts from around the world. They can view videoclips of films, TV shows, and popular music, and they can read the latest theories about media and cyberculture.

FILM

The Titanic

http://members.aol.com/MrScott496/index.html	
Intended Audience	Teachers and students
Grade Level	10-12
Curricular Fit	Film study
Types of Resources	Video and audio clips, reviews, still shots
Authorship of Site	Chris Dohany
Navigation	Good
Visual Appeal	Good
Interactive Activity	Viewing video clips and images, listening to audio clips

There are now available on the Internet thousands of video clips of famous films such as *The Titanic*. We have included one of dozens of *The Titanic* sites here because it is one that is well constructed and would appeal to many adolescents. Sites devoted to blockbuster films such as *The Titanic, Indiana Jones,* or *Jurassic Park* usually contain much interesting material about the film and related information. From the *Jurassic Park* pages, for instance, students can learn not only about the film and Michael Crichton's book, but about chaos theory, genetics, and dinosaurs. The *Indiana Jones* sites link to archeological sites, and from *The Titanic* movie pages you can often go easily to historical data banks about the ship and its passengers. Reading popular culture and decoding the semiotics of films are valuable activities to conduct in a media literacy unit. We recommend, however, that you develop the students' critical literacy about how and why films are constructed as part of the process of teaching them about this medium.

SUGGESTED ACTIVITIES

1. Encourage your students to visit the Luminarium site, where each of them can study a different medieval or Renaissance writer. In their reports to the class they can consider imaginative ways to bring their author's work to life. While reading from Chaucer, for instance, they can learn from the audioclips at the site how to pronounce middle English and then read aloud to their classmates using the appropriate pronunciation. Or they can display images of original illuminated manuscripts.

2. As part of a writer's workshop in which you are encouraging students to edit each other's work and to concentrate upon improving grammatical expression, show them an online grammar website where they can learn how to correct basic sentence errors, usage errors, etc.

3. Take your students to the Poetry Post site to read poems from students around the world and then encourage them to post their own poems at this site.

4. After visiting The Eclectic Writer, The Write Site, and Kid Chronicles with your students, have them try their hand at crime writing, mystery writing, newspaper feature story writing, screen writing, etc. Then have them publish the resulting texts in their own online school newspaper or magazine.

5. Have each of your students read a different speech from the writings of famous women at the Gifts of Speech site. Then encourage them to write speeches of their own in response to the ones which they have read. To guide your students' speech writing, introduce them to the information at the Virtual Presentation Assistant site on effective speech writing and delivery.

6. Ask your students to study the information at the Technology and Learning Online site, and then help them to work together in teams to create multimedia web projects on themes related to your regular course work.

7. Take your ESL students to the Learning English on the Web home page and help them to listen to radio programs or to take part in the language listening lab.

8. Take your students to UNICEF's Voices of Youth site and involve them in a live chat or email conference with children around the world on a human rights issue

such as child labor. Or, through the Epals Classroom Exchange site, connect your whole class with students in a class in another part of the world to carry out a co-operative project based upon the issues raised at UNICEF's site.

9. Involve your students in visiting several school home pages via the Web66 International School Web Site Registry, then have them create or revise your school's home page.

SUMMARY

We have argued throughout this book that developments in technology have obliged teachers to consider a new paradigm for the teaching of language arts. In this final chapter we have made use of the NCTE Standards for the English language arts to organize our presentation of sites and activities. We have indicated, for instance, that, if your goal is to develop in your students "an understanding and respect for diversity," you can accomplish this now by enabling your students to carry out intercultural communication via e-mail with the help of sites such as Epals, Web66, and UNICEF's Voices of Youth. Or if your goal is to help your students to "read literature from many periods," then the Luminarium site can be employed to bring the works of writers such as Chaucer to life through media formats and archives that were not available to language arts teachers even five years ago. We wish you many enjoyable hours of reading and writing adventures as you extend the range and variety of literacy activities that your students can experience thanks to the communicative power of the Internet. We hope that the new vision of English teaching you thus embrace will excite you and your students for years to come.

GLOSSARY

An Internet Language for Easy Surfing

The Internet has its own special language. An understanding of this language is an asset for easy surfing and communicating.

American Standard Code for Information Interchange (ASCII) is format recognized by the computer as containing text and numbers and no graphics.

Archie is a software tool for locating files on *FTP (File Transfer Protocol)* sites. These sites are usually called anonymous FTP sites because a password is not necessary to log into the FTP site for downloading its resources. Log in as anonymous, and your password is your e-mail address.

Bandwidth, in bits per second, is a measure of how much data a modem transfers from one end to another. A fast modem in the 90s has the capacity to transfer or receive up to 30,000 bits per second.

Baud tells how many bits per second a modem can receive or send data. It is the measure of speed of the modem. Bandwith is the measure of quantity. For example, a 2,400 baud modem transfers over 9,600 bits per second of data.

Because It's There Network (BIT-NET) consists of educational sites networked together to form a group outside of the Internet. People in BIT-NET usually run under a *Virtual Memory System (VMS),* the main operating system used in mainframe machines. The BIT-NET is no longer popular.

Binary Hexadecimal (Binhex) is a file that has been converted from a non-ASCII file to an ASCII file. This file is usually used for e-mailing because some e-mail software cannot read non-ASCII e-mail.

Bit is a number that the computer uses, either one or zero, to translate and understand data. It is the smallest unit of measurement in computer data.

Browser is software used to view and extract resources from homepages and Web pages on the Internet. The popular browser programs are Netscape and Microsoft Internet Explorer.

Bulletin Board System (BBS) is an on-line "get-together" system for people to share resources and ideas. A BBS is hosted by an individual or a society. Check your local computer newspaper for the local BBS in your area.

Byte is made up of eight bits. A kilo-byte is 1,024 bytes. A small diskette carries about 1.33 kilobytes.

Common Gateway Interface (CGI) is script-based software, usually written by programmers in *Practical Extraction and Report Language (PERL)*, to in-struct the web server to carry out cer-tain operations. CGI programs/scripts are usually put into a directory called *cgi-bin.*

Cyberspace, coined by William Gib-son, describes the world of the Internet that carries a huge amount of infor-mational resources through computer networks.

Domain, also known as *DNS (Domain Name System)*, personalizes every computer in the world on the Internet. It gives a computer a number or word identification (*www.altavista.com,* for example, is a unique DNS). No two people have the same DNS.

Electronic-Mail (e-mail) is a software tool that is used on the Internet to send text across the Internet from one computer to another simultaneously.

File Transfer Protocol (FTP) is a method used to transfer files from one computer to another. You can use FTP with FTP software such as Fetch or In-ternet browsers.

Frequently Asked Questions (FAQs) is a place where people can look up an-swers to related questions on a partic-ular subject of interest. You can get FAQs on the Internet through personal or commercial infobase Web pages.

Gopher is a traditional way to view and retrieve resources on the Internet. It is menu driven to help you find in-formation resources quickly and effi-ciently. It has no graphic features. For Gopher servers you need Gopher Client software.

Graphics Interchange Format (GIF) is graphic file formatted into GIF classifi-cation. Many of the Internet graphics files are in the GIF format. Another popular graphic format is *jpg,* which is a compressed graphic file.

Homepage is an Internet site reached by an Internet browser. An Internet site starting with *http:// protocol* is called a *homepage* or a *website.*

Host is a computer that provides other computers on the computer networks or the Internet with a variety of ser-vices such as Gopher services, the WWW (World Wide Web), or just printing services.

Hypertext is text that can be linked to other documents by the click of a mouse. Hypertexts are underlined in blue.

HyperText Markup Language (HTML) refers to the computer script-ing language. It is used to make web pages or home pages. HTML docu-ments can usually be recognized by their *htm* or *html* extensions. HTML is used to format and lay out a web page.

HyperText Transport Protocol (HTTP) is used on the Internet to locate hypertext information-based files. Sites with the HTTP protocol are World Wide Web sites.

Inter-Connected-Network (Internet) is a network of computers that share informational resources. Thousands of computers around the world are linked through the Internet to provide and share resource materials.

Internet Protocol Number (IP number) is a number used to identify your computer on the Internet. An IP number on the Internet is equivalent to a social insurance number.

Internet Relay Chat (IRC) is an online live chat environment on the Internet. IRC provides opportunities to communicate and conference with colleagues.

Internet Service Provider (ISP) is an organization that provides access to the Internet for a price.

Intranet is a private, local information-based network, the opposite of Internet. No "outsider" can retrieve data from this network. The network resources are avaliable only to members of the organization.

Listserv is a mailing list that belongs to a group of people with the same interest. Members can share ideas via e-mail.

Local Area Network (LAN) is limited to a specific site or building.

Multipurpose Internet Mail Extensions (MIME) is used as a standard to include non-ASCII files with e-mail messages. Examples of non-ASCII files are sound, movie, and graphic files.

Newsgroup is a service provider for Internet discussions via e-mail. You can post messages on a "news" computer system.

Point-to-Point Protocol (PPP) enables a computer to initiate a normal connection *(TCP/IP)* through a modem and a telephone line to connect to the Internet.

Router is a computer hardware device used to connect two or more networks together.

Server is a computer or software package that initiates and relays all sorts of computer services to network client computers or client software.

Slip stands for *Serial Line Internet Protocol*. It is similar to PPP.

Uniform Resource Locator (URL) is the standard syntax to locate any resource available on the Internet. It is the equivalent of an address for a web site. An example of a URL is *http://home.cc.umanitoba.ca/*.

UNIX is a computer operating system for SUN computers. It is a multi-user computer operating system (DOS and MacOS are examples of simpler computer operating systems).

World Wide Web (WWW) is a subset of the Internet.